Praise

Throw off those blankets and banish your fear! "Don't Play With Fire" is your roadmap to transform your life. We hide from ourselves and take no risks because that makes us feel safe. In fact, taking no risk leaves us just where we are, some of us for the entirety of our lives. Dennis Haber passionately and deftly weaves his life into every aspect of this book and that is what gives it its power. After reading it I committed myself to moving from safety to challenge, and I know already that I have stepped into the place that has been calling to me all along. There is a bright and magical world out there; Dive in, and Dennis will show you how.....it only took me a day to wake up...

BEVERLY BELL

AUTHOR WHISPERS

Imagine there was an individual, who after a lifetime of searching for his purpose, discovered the key secrets of life. These principles have the power to take anyone from a 10 to a 1 on the FEAR scale and from a 1 to a 10 on the CONFIDENCE & ACHIEVEMENT scale. With intense and compelling clarity, Dennis teaches us how to squeeze the most out of life.

JASON FRENN

INTERNATIONAL CONFERENCE SPEAKER & AUTHOR

Take stock of your life and live it to the fullest-it's the only thing that counts. Dennis provides a cutting edge discussion about becoming all that you can be. He convincingly shows that magic happens when you confront reality. My question to you is, Are you ready?

VIKEN MIKAELIAN

CEO, PLANNEDGIVING.COM

With exacting clarity Dennis Haber turns the mind of his reader toward contemplative and life changing thought processes. Apply Dennis Haber's hard won wisdom and learn to love the achiever you become. This short, concise, book is full of "how to" suggestions that work. Read it and grow, you'll be so glad you did!

JULIE ZIGLAR NORMAN
AUTHOR , SPEAKER, REALTOR®, FOUNDER OF ZIGLAR WOMEN,
CEO NORMAN SERVICES CORP.,
VP OF BUSINESS DEVELOPMENT ZIGLAR INC.

I've read a lot of self help books. A lot. This one is different. Really different. If you are longing for a fresh start, a unique approach to life's challenges and victories; this is the book! I can't remember when a book has made me WANT to dig deep and discover simple things that made such a tremendous difference in my life. Read Don't Play With Fire as soon as possible!

CINDY ZIGLAR OATES

Have you ever wondered if you could be, do, or have more in life? The answer is YES, and Dennis Haber shows you exactly how in his inspiring, must-read book Don't Play With Fire: How to Keep Your Greatness from Going Up in Flames. Dennis seamlessly weaves together his own life's experiences with the timeless wisdom of Zig Ziglar to create a practical guide for developing and nurturing your best self. Get out your highlighter and post-it notes; this book is going to become your handbook for achieving the future you've dreamed of!

JENIFER TRUITT
ZIGLAR CERTIFIED COACH AND TRAINER

DON'T PLAY WITH FIRE

How to Keep Your Greatness from Going Up in Flames

Dennis Haber

DHCM Media Group, Inc.

DON'T PLAY WITH FIRE: How to Keep Your Greatness from Going Up in Flames

Copyright ©2018 Dennis Haber

All rights reserved.

No part of this publication may be reproduced, stored in a retrieval system or transmitted in any form or by any means, electronic, mechanical, photocopying, recording or otherwise without written permission, except in the case of brief quotations embodied in articles or reviews.

Written permission may be obtained by contacting the author at dennis@dennishaber.com.

This publication provides personal information and anecdotal situations that are not intended as legal, financial, or professional advice on the part of the author and publisher.

Published by DHCM Media Group, Inc.

ISBN: 978-0-9898919-3-6

Printed in the United States of America.

Interior and cover design by: Jan Guarino/Guarino Graphics

*To Shelley,
Jason and Cory*

Contents

Foreword by Tom Ziglar	11
Introduction — Create a Hopeful Future	12
1 Be in Learning Mode	17
2 Make Adversity Your Friend	27
3 Communicate More Effectively	35
4 Reject Negative Thoughts	47
5 Defend Against "Attitude Sclerosis"	61
6 Stop Wasting Time and Put Your Thoughts into Action	71
7 Know How to Plan	81
8 Optimize Your Important Relationships	89
9 Develop Sharper Insights	101
10 Be in Charge of You	115
11 Understand the Origin of Fear	125
12 Do Life Differently	135
13 Claim Your Greatness	143
My Favorite Zig Ziglar "Principles of Life"	150
Acknowledgments	152
About the Author	154

Foreword

This book is about desire, hope, grit, and ropes. As you read this book, let me give you a framework you can use to get the most out of it so that it can get the most out of you. Imagine, if you will, that you are on a journey, the journey of life, and the vehicle you are taking to your destination is a beautiful hot air balloon that can take you over the toughest obstacles and give you the greatest view.

Desire is the bucket of the balloon where you enjoy the ride and the view. You have to have clarity on where you are going - what do you really desire? And you have to understand your unique gifts, talents, strengths, and skills that you pack into the bucket with you. Once your desire gets lit up with clarity, it begins to fuel the balloon of hope.

Hope allows you to see the future as it can be, the future that you were created for! As the balloon begins to rise, your view gets better and gives you even more clarity on your desires, dreams, and goals. Now you need white-hot fuel - we call this grit.

Grit is the furnace of your balloon. If you want your balloon to gain altitude and take you across the oceans and the mountains of your life, you need to work on your gifts, talents, strengths, and skills with grit. Grit means you persevere through the tough times and you keep on working no matter the circumstances. If you get knocked down a hundred times, you get up 101 times. Your balloon gains altitude and momentum fast when you apply grit! But did you remember to cut the ropes?

Ropes are what tie your balloon to the ground. Have you ever been at a point in your life where all systems were go, you took off, only to suddenly get jerked to a stop? You need to cut the ropes! Ropes can be many things: Bad habits, wrong mindsets, lack of knowledge or wise counsel, the wrong input. Whatever is holding you back.

Dennis does a masterful job showing you exactly how to cut the ropes, develop your gifts and talents with grit, clarify your desires, and take your hope to an incredible altitude so that you can become all that God created you to become.

Enjoy the journey. The view is incredible!

Tom Ziglar
CEO of Ziglar Inc.

Introduction

CREATE A HOPEFUL FUTURE

Life can sometimes resemble a raging, out of control fire. This occurs whenever your emotions lay waste to everything in its path. As hopes and dreams are decimated, you fear all is lost. Overwhelmed and exhausted, you realize you are in need of help. If you are tired of being sick and tired about your life, don't despair. Help is on the way.

Whether you are looking for transformational change, are simply curious about seeking a different path, or are concerned about current predicaments, there is critical information waiting for you within this book. No matter what you are looking to achieve, you can learn how to squeeze more out of your life.

Don't Play With Fire helps you go deep inside yourself to re-establish discipline and re-gain control. Another goal is to help you interact with others in rewarding and fruitful ways. Living life is not just about retaining control over your mind and self; it is also about optimizing your relationships with others. I suggest you use these ideas and tools as soon as possible. Once you begin to implement them into your daily habits you will experience a huge difference in your personal, business and family affairs.

When you accept the fact that you are the only person holding you back, you can unleash wisdom by expanding your perceptions of newly discovered abilities. One year from now, when you look back upon your accomplishments, you will see that your life has become much more than 365 days of reruns.

The book begins with the concept of learning because that is the one thing you can do each day of your life. You can read books, attend lectures and seminars and listen to podcasts. You can also keep a notebook handy to dutifully examine your day each evening. This will help you determine where you need to do better.

Living in a state of perpetual learning is transformative. It enhances self-esteem and confidence. It forces you to ponder how and why you do certain things, puts you on a path to build new mental maps and improves your ability to analyze problems. It becomes an ongoing opportunity to re-evaluate your thoughts and beliefs.

For me, this has been an ongoing process. For years, I kept a journal of my personal and business activities. This exercise was rather instructive, as I studied and compared reactions and responses to situations I encountered. Each evening, I would evaluate and grade myself. I learned a lot by thinking over alternative approaches I could have chosen. Eventually, this exercise equipped me to be and do better, to understand who I was, what I was doing right, what I was doing wrong and what measures I could take to improve. The insight from this exercise spilled over into all areas of my life. Constant self-examination allowed me to become a better employer, colleague and friend, as well as a more responsible and loving husband and father.

One evening, this journal developed a life of its own. As the words came gushing forth, I was amazed. Events long forgotten, including old wounds, were vividly re-created and I was stunned when I realized I had usually played the victim. Through writing, I caught a glimpse of the real me, or at least what the real me could be. This time, as I pondered previous events in my life, I saw a series of lessons I needed to learn. As I continued to write and transcribe my journal into a first draft of a book, I kept focusing on filling it with actionable, clear and direct advice. Because I was so busy with my career and family, the original draft languished for nearly two decades before I finally found time to update and revise its content. I must admit it was quite a struggle. There were times I felt lost, unsure which way to turn. One of the hardest things to do in life is to persevere in the struggle to find your north star. Words, thoughts and actions can be so powerful. They can provide ah-ha moments of discovery. These insights, when I chose to trust them, inevitably guided me back in the right direction. Not surprisingly, when I finally completed what you are reading now, it bore little relationship to the original.

I also found that exposing secret thoughts entails a fair

amount of risk. Sometimes, it was hard to determine which personal experiences should be trumpeted and which should remain invisible. But I was ready to dig deep to find my lost treasure—my purpose in life.

Have you ever noticed that treasure is never buried in shallow ground? It is always buried deep down and requires heavy excavation. Perhaps the burning desire to discover this purpose far outweighed the risk of exposure.

One day last summer, I sat at my desk, wondering how I could be most productive with the rest of my life. Three things were a given: I enjoy writing. I enjoy public speaking. I feel complete when I am of service to others. I eventually discovered that I could become certified as a trainer and "life coach" by the iconic Ziglar organization.

My second act in life, as a Ziglar Legacy Certified Trainer and Ziglar Legacy Certified Coach, is dedicated to helping people find their greatness so that they can become the person they wish to be.

I have poured my heart and soul into this book. Having faced some mighty personal battles of my own, the principles in this book have been my weapon. During my childhood, I didn't know these weapons existed. And as I grew older, I sometimes misplaced them, but now they make each day meaningful and fulfilling. Now, I offer each of them to you.

Throughout the book, you will find tools to assist you in your quest to become a bigger and better person in all facets of your life. By looking honestly at yourself in a mirror, you can glimpse at those areas in need of improvement. It is only when you develop the courage to peek *inside,* that you will finally discover what is really hiding under your *personal hood.*

Each chapter contains a relevant part of my personal story. They demonstrate how the noted concepts and principles eventually won out over my ignorance. These tools helped me get back on track after many unintended detours.

If I was able to get back on track, you can certainly do the same for yourself and for your family.

Each chapter initially concludes by asking a central question:

Are you a *flamethrower* or a *fire extinguisher*? This salient question highlights the central point of the chapter.

A person who is a *flamethrower* causes hurt and pain - to himself and others. A person who is a *fire extinguisher* protects and makes things better.

This is followed by a *Contemplation Page,* where you have space to ponder your own struggles. Additionally, you can write down answers to accompanying end of chapter questions that will help you reflect upon what you have just learned, as you consider your next best moves.

As you prepare to begin, I must warn you that the ride can get bumpy at times, as you earnestly examine your life's journey. At long last, you are about to find your buried treasure, just like I did. My wish for you is that you find yours today rather than tomorrow. Once you make these concepts, ideas and principles part of your life, it will become richer and more blessed.

– Dennis Haber
Long Island, New York

CHAPTER ONE
BE IN LEARNING MODE

You will make a lousy anybody else, but you will be the best "you" in existence.

Zig Ziglar

LIFE IS A CLASSROOM. Those who choose to ignore this truth, do so at their peril. You'll always need additional knowledge. I'm not suggesting that you need to earn more diplomas and degrees. What I am suggesting is that you must always be on the lookout for learning opportunities. When you are, your life will get better and better.

Are You a "Know-It-All?"
You may believe that you have already learned it all. After all, that's why you went to school. "There is nothing else to learn," I've heard some people say.

If this is your attitude, the fulfillment of your life's dreams will remain an empty, meaningless wish. To achieve the most, your mind must be on a never-ending search for new solutions and patterns of thought. A person open to new perspectives is always welcoming all possibilities and wonders. For them, learning is a perpetual, daily experience. After all, your teachers are everywhere and life's situations make the best classrooms. Are you taking advantage of these opportunities?

Once you understand this learning paradigm, the self-flagellation for missed opportunities will cease. You will realize that if you treat every error, every mistake, every silly experience as a learning experience, instead of a reason to insult and degrade yourself, your life will be richer and more meaningful. Therefore, turn every negative into a positive. Stop saying, *"If only I did this"* or *"If only I did that."* This mindset will keep you stuck in the quagmire of self-doubt. Now say, *"Next Time I Will."* Become that perpetual student and you too will quickly advance to the head of the class.

Mr. Ziglar taught that it is important to learn from your past without living there; it is just as important to seize each moment you can in the present. He concludes that it is also critical to look into your future with hope. It all starts with learning.

"Next Time I Will"

A look into the world of sports provides some excellent examples of people who have rebounded from their mistakes and refused to be defined by a single event. In effect, they said *"Next Time I Will."* For example, Michael Jordan was cut from his high school basketball team and came to be considered the greatest basketball player to have ever played the game. Chris Webber made one of the most colossal mistakes in college basketball history. While playing as a freshman for the University of Michigan, he cost his team a win in the national championship game by calling a timeout when his team had none left. Yet, the following year he became Rookie of the Year in the NBA. Jordan Spieth lost the 2016 Masters golf tournament after securing a 5 shot lead, with only nine holes to play. Yet, by the age of 23, he won three major tournaments. The only other player to accomplish this was the great Jack Nicklaus. In 1986, Greg Norman had the lead in all four majors going into the final round and won only once. Yet he was voted into the World Golf Hall of Fame in 2001 and is one of the savviest businessmen in the golfing world today.

Here are some other *Next Time I Will* folks: R.H. Macy failed seven times before creating the Macy's retail chain. Walt Disney was told that he lacked imagination and was fired from a Missouri newspaper. Albert Einstein's teachers thought he was mentally handicapped and Thomas Edison was told he was too stupid to learn anything.

When you commit yourself to *Next Time I Will* thinking, you will discover added benefits. No longer will you lose control when a presentation goes poorly. You will stop kicking yourself when you say the wrong thing at the wrong time. No longer will you get upset when you make a wrong turn and arrive late.

Starting today, you will learn from experience. As a result, you will improve faster and have less stress because you will be in constant *learning mode*. The mistake, snafu, error, or blunder will be palpable for all to see, except now they will no longer cause you hurt and grief. Having this mindset means that you already know that partaking in any activity includes the chance of making mistakes. There's an added benefit when you take this approach. You will also become aware of and learn from the blunders of others.

This lesson will free you from the perfectionist trap that is so easy to fall into. In fact, perfectionism is often an excuse to not try at all—simply because you may fail.

Learn from *All* Your Experiences
Doctors, researchers and scientists learn through trial and error. The world will be forever indebted to pioneers like Dr. Christian Barnard, who in 1967 transplanted the heart of a 24-year-old woman into a 55-year-old male patient and to Dr. Tom Starzl, who performed the first successful liver transplant that same year. Imagine if they berated and chastised themselves after every surgical failure and told themselves how stupid they were. What would they have accomplished?

Get the point? People who have changed the world for the better have taught us something more precious than any discovery they made. They have shown us that with the right approach, you can create the freedom to become the person you always wanted to be and to do the things you always wished to do. Perhaps this is exactly why doctors are said to be *practicing medicine*. They knew so much time and effort would have been wasted if they did not learn from their mistakes.

Say Goodbye to Your Past
When you make this shift into *learning mode*, the most amazing things will happen. Your past will no longer hold you back. You will welcome constructive criticism. Your relationships will improve and you will view yourself in a more positive way. You will discover that your errors and the errors of others now have a singular purpose: To make you better in every way.

In effect, you will give birth to your true self. This is a most exciting possibility and once you decide to make this important shift your critiques of others will contain helpful and insightful solutions. You will no longer have the need or the desire to harshly criticize anyone.

Empirical data indicates that many people refrain from taking action because they are stuck in the past. They wrongly believe that their past represents their future. However, the past is just a snapshot of what happened before. You can control your future by learning from your past, not by leaning on your past, as Mr. Ziglar taught.

Picture your favorite baseball team playing a crucial night game. Your team is behind. That is the bad news. The good news is, the bases are loaded in the bottom of the ninth. Because of an injury, a pinch hitter is coming to the plate, a rookie, batting for the first time in his major-league career. Unfortunately, he strikes out and your team loses. But, this does not mean he will strike out each time he subsequently comes to bat. It's up to him how he handles the situation.

How will he react? Will he be like many others we know, who fear that an initial error, bad move, or mistake in their personal, business, or family life will be repeated? Because of diminished confidence, many believe they will continually strike out each time they come to the plate in the game of life.

Let's sneak a peek at his next game when our rookie comes up to the plate for his second at-bat. The circumstances are eerily similar. His past cannot be rewritten. Last night, he struck out for the final out. This time he got a hit, which won the game.

It is important to note that his past was relevant only if he let it define his ability. Do not let a disappointing past control your future. Even if you *struck out* at something you recently attempted, tomorrow will provide you with another opportunity to get a hit. So, whether you need another chance to reset things with your spouse, boss, client, kids, friends or significant other, you will always have that opportunity, providing you let your past be your teacher.

Reframing a Mistake as a Success

Did you know that blackboards in school were really invented so that your errors and mistakes could be erased? It's a good idea to carry that process with you in your mind's eye because it is guaranteed that you will become more confident when you learn from your mistakes and turn them into successes. Once you see that process in action, you can erase any actual reminder of a mistake from your memory, just as you would erase it from the blackboard. By doing so, you can reframe what seemed like a negative into a positive.

This type of learning takes you past the limits of your ignorance into a place called accomplishment. You cannot realize your sincerest hopes and dreams by ignoring this learning paradigm. If you start right now, your life will immediately change. It is like rubbing a genie's lamp and asking the genie to grant you three wishes. It is that simple.

MY STORY

My love affair with real estate started in the 1970s while I was in college and took a job as a real estate agent. I wasn't trained very well but I did the best I could. I worked many weekends without a single sale. Then one weekend, it happened: I sold two homes. I was ecstatic!

For many weeks, I played the tour guide. "This is the bathroom and there's the kitchen."

Everyone on the house tour knew what room we were in, but this was what I was taught to do. One weekend, I took a couple to view several homes. The wife asked many questions. Once she realized I didn't have any answers, she started yelling at me until she was screaming at the top of her lungs. I couldn't blame her one bit. She was trying to get pertinent facts from her agent and he (me) was not capable of offering any help.

A light bulb went off in my head that day. I knew that if my boss, or anyone else, wasn't going to provide me with the tools I needed to succeed, then I would have to do it myself.

It was all up to me. In college, I concentrated on my own self-improvement. My friend Richie's dad gave me *How To Win Friends and Influence People*, the iconic book by Dale Carnegie. It's essentially about hope, which I learned is much more than just a word. It is a state of mind. It resides within each of us. It can be a power that others see and sense in us. It is like a mentor whispering in your ear, "Go ahead; you can do it!" And you do.

Carnegie's book was my first encounter with the world of self-improvement. I loved it and I have been devouring books, tapes and CDs on the subject ever since.

In my second year of law school at the University of Akron, I won the American Jurisprudence Award for the study of Corporate Law. This course lasted 20 weeks, which was twice as long as any other course. The law professor's final exam was also quite different and I knew I needed to devise a different study strategy. Each week, I studied the current work and reviewed the past chapters. When it came time to take the exam, I knew the material like the back of my hand. I stayed calm and self-assured. Unlike my years in the public school system, I was gaining confidence.

When I became a lawyer, I primarily practiced real estate law. I went to seminars and constantly talked with my peers about best practices. I was always updating my knowledge, which meant my success was directly tied to being in perpetual *learning mode*. I retained this mindset when I entered the mortgage business and began investing in real estate. It was also relevant for me when I transitioned into the non-profit world of real estate donations with my esteemed colleague, Chase Magnuson.

Many years ago, I was given wise advice—to seek out opportunities to speak in public and to write articles for publications. It is only by speaking and writing about a topic that you learn just how well you know a subject.

When I first spoke in public I did so many things wrong: I didn't consider the make-up of the audience; flaunted my perceived intelligence; talked past my aloted time, so I wouldn't have to take questions and didn't engage the audience.

Over time, I became a lot better. I corrected these mistakes and gained confidence. Eventually, I helped others who wished to venture into public speaking. A short time ago, I completed the Ziglar Speakers Institute, because I wanted to improve my keynote addresses.

I never stopped learning. Writing articles, like public speaking, requires that you know your material cold and requires that you guide your readers through a pre-determined, cogent path. When I started writing and speaking for public consumption, the specter of criticism unnerved me. Over time, I became more comfortable expressing myself and accepting the opinions of others. Remember, that the goal is to always get better and improve.

Having the ability to write and speak can often be a differentiating factor in a competitive world. Often the only way to get noticed and get to the next level is to remain in learning mode. Are you committed to doing that?

Are you a flamethrower or a fire extinguisher?
Flamethrower:
When something happens and you say, *"If Only I,"* chances are you will remain stuck in the past. The only thing that you'll learn is how to remain a victim.

Fire Extinguisher:
When you say, *"Next Time I Will"* you are moving past the event and figuring out how to best respond next time. This is the quintessential example of being in learning mode.

Contemplation Page

How would prior events in your life have changed if the Learning Paradigm was already a part of your arsenal?

....
....
....
....
....

How can you use the criticism received from your spouse, boss, relative, or friend to improve your life?

....
....
....
....
....

With this learning shift securely in place, how and when will you reach new levels of accomplishment and achievement?

....
....
....
....
....

CHAPTER 2

MAKE ADVERSITY YOUR FRIEND

*The door to a balanced success
opens widest on the hinges of
hope and encouragement*
ZIG ZIGLAR

NAVIGATING THROUGH LIFE'S PEAKS AND VALLEYS

can be a challenge. Sooner or later, everyone will come face-to-face with adversity. Confronting new threats takes discipline. Life has so many moving parts—personal experiences, business dealings and family dynamics— all are constantly in flux. There will always be ups and downs. Some will be exceedingly good and others quite bad. It is the tough moments which leave an indelible mark and unfortunately define one's path. You, however, have a choice. You can make adversity a friend or an enemy. If you choose to make it a friend, you will have the needed strength, courage and grit to improve your current situation and circumstance. After taking that initial deep breathe of regret that this event happened, you'll be able to see what clearly needs to be done and take appropriate action. The depth of the struggle will ultimately determine the extent of your growth. However, when you choose to make adversity the enemy, you will resist that which has already occurred and be relegated to playing the victim. It is futile to resist something which has become reality.

John D Rockefeller called the Panic of 1857, his "school of adversity." Until that time, it was the greatest economic depression our country had ever experienced. When you can harness a learning moment out of travesty, like Rockefeller did, the gift of education— learning moments, permits you to see what others refuse to see. He viewed an obstacle as a disguised opportunity. When adversity rears its ugly head there are three things you can do: 1. Keep emotions in check and do not panic. 2. Focus on controllable factors, which include your emotions, attitudes, awareness and judgments. 3. Look for the good in every experience and situation.

Choosing Light Over Darkness
While playing the victim role, you'll become a prisoner to your mind. Defeatist thoughts will restrict you as if you were housed in a maximum security facility. The goal here, is to provide you with the strength to break free. It is imperative to acknowledge and trust your abilities. This requires that you stop resisting what has happened and start embracing what is. In other words, take action. Make a move.

Gather some momentum. You'll be glad you finally stopped being a spectator. Reclaiming control over your life is priority number one. Adversity breaks some people. Those who confront it, clobber it, and conquer it break records. Whenever you can break free from those internal and external constraints, you are making mighty progress. The sooner you take the steps to deal with the issue at hand, the quicker your life will take positive shape. In fact, achieving greatness may not be as far away as you think.

Moving forward with positive action will allow you to discover that you are responsible for creating your reality. This realization will act as a salve that will soothe any hatred, anger and hostility.

This is not to say that there will not be backward steps. There will be. Any attempt at change means you are leaving one part of yourself behind as you try to define another part of yourself. It is a process and it usually happens through small steps. However, you don't have to forget the parts you left behind, because they will always be a part of you.

Seeing Adversity as Opportunity
Genuine improvement only occurs when adversity is confronted head on. Children must learn this lesson as early as possible. Sadly, many do not. For example, many parents panic when their child does not receive what they consider to be a good report card, or prematurely panic when they fear that a good grade may not be obtained. The child is punished or threatened with negative consequences. Meaningful discussions about how parents can help or what a child needs to do differently are often never considered. The child's poor grades no longer define conversation between parent and child. Punishment erects its own set of communication and behavioral barriers. On the other hand, a promised reward for a good grade can quickly turn into a punishment when the grade is not good enough to meet parental expectations. When grades do not improve, there is no failsafe program to help the child.

The reward/punishment cycle teaches children the wrong lesson. "If you want me to do better, then promise me something, like a bigger allowance." This thought deemphasizes the love of learning. It teaches that enriching the wallet is better than enriching the mind. It typically prevents the parent from offering sound encouragement. It also fails to get the point across that a poor result can be overcome with hard work. As a result, "I can't" thinking dominates "I can" thinking. Such reasoning forestalls the pleasure of learning and can sometimes prevent children from becoming self-motivating adults.

A Path to Self-Esteem
When you embrace adversity, you'll have more opportunity for insight, as you choose how to interpret life's lessons and deal with its accompanying consequences. The degree of grace you welcome into your life will be meaningful. Regardless, you must become astute and skillful as you navigate your way through life's bumpy roads. Understanding the cumulative meaning and effects of your thoughts, beliefs, words and actions is a critical step as you finally take complete control over your destiny.

MY STORY
I remember the first time I learned about the solar system, that earth was the third planet from the sun. If I'm here, it didn't make sense that Earth is there revolving around the sun. I felt a real disconnect between *the here* and *the there*, which was profoundly similar at the time to my understanding of life. I found it rather difficult to connect the dots because I believed that life should be a smooth endeavor, like ice-skating. Just as one glides over the ice, one should glide through life. People were born so they could enjoy and love life. I discovered the hard way that it doesn't quite work this way, that a smooth sea never produces an experienced sailor.

During my sophomore year in high school, I got my first job as a counter person in a neighborhood cleaner. Things did not go very well. Everything I did seemed wrong. I lasted a couple of hours before I was fired, which was personally devastating and quite embarrassing. I remember telling friends that the owner didn't know what he was doing and I didn't deserve to be fired.

That wasn't the only time I thought I knew better than the adult in charge. After writing a huge paper on World War II, I couldn't believe it when Mr. Trepcos, my social studies teacher, gave me a "C". After spending numerous hours in the library doing all the appropriate research and hitting all the major points, I was convinced beyond any doubt that I would receive an "A" for the finest paper I had ever written. I was certain that Mr. Trepcos must have made a mistake, but he insisted that none had been made, which prompted our own little battle.

He told me there were so many spelling errors it took the joy out of reading the paper.

"Who cares about spelling errors?" I said. "The content was complete and compelling."

I lost the battle on two counts: I ignored his perspective and didn't learn anything from this outcome.

My first job experience and the social studies paper illustrate missed opportunities for improving future performance. When I failed to hold myself accountable, I missed a chance to become better. I could not figure things out at the time and did not learn.

I have heard life described as a pinball machine. Like the little silver ball, you get bounced around, ricocheting from one spot (life situation) to another, with little control over the result. Eventually, one game ends and another begins, with the bouncing and ricocheting happening all over again.

If you agree with this metaphor, you'll resign yourself to a hopeless, continuous loop of powerlessness. Wondering how things spiraled out of control will be commonplace. However, when you become proactive, you can instead review how you contributed to the actual outcome. It takes courage and strength to identify shortcomings. When you are able to do this, you can focus upon your next moves.

As closing counsel, I represented many lenders and financial institutions. Earlier in my career, I received a wake-up jolt when my biggest lending client merged with a larger FDIC bank. This meant that my volume of closings decreased because other law firms, which already represented this lender, received the additional business. Adversity teaches you that you never have enough business. I learned the hard way that the best time to market oneself is during good times. It's too late when bad times have already struck.

Never forget that you always have a next move. This is a great lesson to learn in your personal, business and family life. Adversity always provides a reason for a next move, a next step and that's what I always look for—the next best move. You also have a next best move. Do you see it?

Are you a flamethrower or a fire extinguisher?
Flamethrower:
When you resist some event that has already occurred you will become a victim. Your resistance will prevent you from doing anything constructive.

Fire Extinguisher:
Examine any adverse circumstance you find yourself in and then determine what your next best step will be.

Contemplation Page

Why do you still refuse to acknowledge or resist adverse situations when they occur?

Are there areas in your life you feel powerless to change? If so, list them and explain why.

What different thoughts will you have the next time you face *adversity*?

CHAPTER 3
COMMUNICATE MORE EFFECTIVELY

What comes out of your mouth is determined by what goes into your mind

Zig Ziglar

When I think about communication, I'm reminded of a game we played as kids—*The Tapper and The Listener.* In this game, the tapper would tap out the rhythm of a song and it was the job of the listener to guess its name. I remember how frustrated I would get when the listener couldn't guess the song because meanwhile, I was humming away or singing the words to myself, not believing that the listener couldn't name the song. It was so obvious to me, but not for the listener.

Communication is similar. You know the point you want to convey and you do so, but the listener may be hearing quite a different tune.

Many things impact the quality of comprehension—the way the communication is sent, the choice of words, actions that may accompany the words, the need for instant gratification, labeling, asking questions and the two-sided problem influence. I'm referring here to the media's predisposition for presenting only two sides of an issue.

The Secret Ingredient

Listening is the engine through which effective communication occurs. It provides an opportunity to understand the meaning and feeling behind the speaker's words. Listening includes understanding non-verbal cues. A pause can provide time for a thought to sink in. A gesture with the arms, hands, body, or face can provide nuance. The voice can be used to emphasize a point. Robert Bolton, in his book, *People Skills,* reminds us that communication requires a bit of detective work. Those who seek to actively understand the speaker will have a great advantage. Therefore, face-to-face communication is better at creating lasting and stronger relationships in business and in the home. Important issues should rarely be resolved through online communication.

Today, however, it certainly seems as if more individuals prefer communicating through their smartphones and tablets. This is having a negative effect on establishing deep relationships. Important non-verbal clues can't be considered. While it is true that these devices are helping individuals become better organized and focused, they can never be a substitute for establishing strong and lasting face-to-face relationships.

Mr. Ziglar points out in his book, *Born to Win,* that modern American society has become rude and self-centered. The abiding attitude is "Hooray for me and to heck with you."

Effective face-to-face communication is dependent upon understanding the meaning behind verbal and non-verbal cues. Words and word inflection become quite significate in the interpretation of an expressed thought. The written word, on the other hand, lacks emotional nuance. When you comprehend this difference, you will more likely choose your words carefully and avoid inflammatory remarks when using your devices.

Interactive Listening and Communication Erases All Doubt
As a speaker, I know the message I want to convey. As the words flow from my mouth, the recipient must interpret them. A good listener will take what is heard, rephrase it and throw it back to the speaker for validation. This interactive form of communication offers the listener an opportunity to confirm his or her interpretation of what was said. If necessary, the speaker has an opportunity to correct the interpretation.

Interactive listening and communication can be quite effective when properly used. It can filter out communication clutter and noise, isolate meaning and detect feeling and concern. Comprehension skills will measurably improve.

It bears repeating that online communication is not a substitute for face-to-face dialogue. While it does provide an increase in community conversation, correspondence and sense of belonging, these community bonds are rather weak. The sharing of similar viewpoints generally preclude exposure to diverse views and opinions. People prefer that their online buddies supply affirmation of their collective thoughts. Social media greatly enhances this confirmation bias.

Effective face-to-face and online communication is further reduced when the listener is too busy fashioning a reply to what is being communicated. The lost art of listening and understanding is affecting the cohesiveness of every relationship, whether personal or professional. People have trouble on the job and in the home because they lack the ability to listen, comprehend and appropriately express themselves in a meaningful way.

> In those instances, it is helpful to pause and ask yourself two key questions.
> Do I really have to express those words right now?
> Are there other words or thoughts I can use to calm the situation?

Your answers can make all the difference in the outcome of your exchanges. Remember: Kind words do not cost much, but unkind words can be quite expensive.

Words Have Consequences

In a civilized society, words are the weapon of choice. They can maim and cause long-lasting injuries, even to the sender. For example, it is probably not a good idea to post that you intend to use all of your leftover sick days and then quit your job. It is also not a good idea to post that your new job requires a perfunctory drug test and then ask if anyone knows how to pass a drug test. It's probably not a good idea to post that you want to harm your boss or another employee. Yet people have done each of these things online.

If people can harm themselves, they can certainly aim their venom at others and they do on a steady basis. At the other end of the spectrum, the sender seems not to care about the effects words have on the recipient. This is why bullying is more persistent online. It used to be that the victim of bullying wanted to just get away from their small group of tormentors. Now, that online group could multiply quite quickly.

The Difficulty of Online Communication

To underscore the difficulty with online communication, it is important to note the all-too-frequent stories of family members or friends communicating online. All seems well until someone intentionally inflicts injury upon oneself or upon others. In these instances, we see that without face-to-face communication, things can go seriously wrong.

Body language makes up 55 percent of human comprehension. Tone of voice makes up 38 percent. The actual words we use make up only 7 percent of effective comprehension.

Social media has brought us into a different kind of world. Instead of receiving one's undivided attention, one gets partial attention, at best. The next time you are in a restaurant or another public place, watch how many people are focusing more on their phones than on face-to-face conversation. It is astounding to watch.

In our instant gratification world, people find it difficult to hold back from expressing their immediate thoughts, whether appropriate or not. The words just fly out into a somewhat unknown web of social media. Today, the easiest thing to do is to ridicule, condemn and find fault. There appears to be a lack of understanding of what human interaction is really about. All too often, strings and threads of emails continue past a point where the content is effective. It seems the uber-tactic of many people is to have the last word.

Looking at alternatives to solve an issue is a strategy. Identifying the key problem or problems is a strategy. Having the last word is not a strategy.

How the Media Influences the Way We Communicate

The media has a disproportionate influence on our communication. For example, because they need to constantly grab our attention, the media always highlight the conflict angle. Discussion features opposing groups, usually two opposing forces facing each other. This makes the story, whether it's a news show, expose´ or article, extremely marketable.

It could then be called "The Battle of" or "The War Between." Many headlines also contain the words — *conflict, assault or combat*. While concepts sell better when there are two diametrically opposing forces, the public can be fooled into thinking they are becoming educated. After all, they are receiving both sides of the issue.

We become content with the illusion that we are open minded and that we have done our job by examining both sides of an issue. But are there always just two sides to an issue? Can there be only one, or many? Of course! The media, however, doesn't often see it that way. The best illustration of a one-sided issue is the Holocaust. It is a known event because of the colossal amount of evidence attesting to its existence. Yet today, there are still programs aired and articles written claiming that it didn't happen.

You may mimic the media and always try to present the pros and cons of an issue. It seems fashionable these days to stand firm on a position taken. The two-sided issue has imbued our thinking. A third alternative side is rarely considered. This is one reason why you typically do not widen your search for additional options. You are comfortable just looking for two sides to an issue, notwithstanding that there could be three, four, or five alternative perspectives. Answers and conclusions regarding your own life can be missed when you hold to a narrow, two-sides-only view.

The Problem with Labeling

The labeling problem is becoming more common. Again, many take their cue from the media, as they love to place labels on ideas and people. One is a liberal or conservative, Republican, Democrat, or Independent, gay or lesbian—on and on it goes. This approach is emulated all too frequently. Start listening for when you and someone else—a boss, friend, spouse, colleague, or family member—fall into this insidious trap. The labeled person is not looked upon as an individual with a viewpoint, but as a thing to be labeled and discarded.

The act of labeling can also hurt you. Let's use an imaginary individual to make the point. Jerry Sosa is considered by senior management to be the most articulate and imaginative rising executive in the company. A major position has just become vacant. The company decided that there are only two possible candidates for this position: Jerry Sosa and you.

The executive committee will conduct a series of interviews with the two candidates. You have known Jerry Sosa for five years. If you agree with the initial assessment of the committee, you too will label him brilliant and give yourself little chance to succeed. When you walk into the room your body will be doing most of the talking. It will be shouting, "I'm not as good as Jerry Sosa." However, if you label him just worthy, you are placing him on an even keel with yourself. You recognize his talent. You also recognize your talent. Labeling him *worthy* will allow you to walk into the room with confidence.

If, on the other hand, you consider Jerry Sosa to be a know-nothing, smooth-talking opportunist with no special talent, you will not be in awe of him the way the committee is. But whether you call him brilliant, worthy, or a know-nothing, is it not the same Jerry Sosa you are talking about? You and only you, determine the degree of power you grant him. Perhaps the better choice may be not to label Jerry Sosa at all.

You will always face opponents who look better, dress better, or talk better. You will always come up against people who excel in areas you do not. Your power comes in knowing that this is quite all right. True power is being your authentic self and knowing that it is important to learn from each experience.

Being someone you are not will never provide you with power. When you go into a meeting, be yourself. Give it your best shot. Prepare in an appropriate way. When the meeting is over, evaluate what happened in an honest way. When the result becomes known, get feedback from the participants.

Labeling is for those who seek to dominate others and for those who give up prematurely to play the victim. You on the other hand, would rather be on a different path: A winner's path.

Let's also assume that our Mr. Sosa has the appropriate pedigree. He went to the right schools and has some advanced degrees. However, he doesn't have your vast practical and/or technical experience. If the committee preferred experience over pedigree, you could have talked the committee out of choosing you because of your poor performance.

Questions Are Your Friends
Who, What, When, Where, Why and How are the best six friends that you will ever have. Together, they provide the tools to identify problems and create possible solutions. Yet, too often, these friends are ignored.

I bet you can remember the time, in class or in a meeting, when you purposely refrained from asking a particular question.

Instead, the person next to you asked the exact question. You probably said to yourself, "Gee, that was my question." To add insult to injury, that person was recognized for having insight.

Let's go back to a previous concept we talked about: Learn from experience. Find comfort in knowing that there is no such thing as a stupid question. The reason this is true is because you have created a learning paradigm. Accordingly, your goal as a truth-seeker is to become wiser faster. So, don't be afraid to ask questions of yourself and of others.

Here are some initial soul-searching questions you may wish to consider:

Who is on your side and who should be on your side?
What do people say about you when you are not present?
When do you want to start improving your life situation?
Where do you want to be in six months, a year or in three years—in your personal life, business life and family life?
Why do you keep people in your inner circle who continuously tear you down?
How do you see your self-image today?

Here are a few more:

Who inspires you?
What makes you come alive?
When should you remain silent instead of asserting yourself?
When should you assert yourself instead of remaining silent?
Where can you find solutions to your problems?
Why isn't this (fill in the blank) working?
How can you reach your goals?

MY STORY

There was a time I was looking for a paralegal to assist me with real estate closings. Among other things, my firm represented many lending institutions. I had interviewed several people. I scoured countless resumes but had not found the right person, until Gene walked through the door. Gene was a retired corrections officer and was as gentle as he was big. We talked for a while before I concluded that he would not be a good fit because he didn't have the experience I thought he needed. As he was about to leave, he said, "Give me a chance. I won't let you down." After he left, I couldn't get his words out of my head. He spoke with such conviction. He meant every word he said. I could have labeled him, a corrections officer and not fit for this work. Instead, I hired him and he became known in the industry as Gene the Closing Machine.

When I was elected to the Student Faculty Senate at Adelphi University, I was silenced by the intimidation of having to face the faculty and by the fear of asking a question they would deem stupid. The faculty made it clear, at least in my mind, that they did not treat students as equals. This was my intimidation and mine only. I was constantly upset when someone else asked the very same question I would have asked, but couldn't.

After finally graduating from Akron University School of Law (more on that later) and passing the New York State Bar Exam, I was pumped to find my first law job. I had my feelers out. I spoke to family and friends, hoping someone would know of a firm looking to hire eager talent. I also sent out resumes. The job market was not good. I was uber-excited when an attorney contacted me and I had several interviews with him. Each time I was called back, I became more confident I would be hired. He finally said, "I'll let you know in a few days." When he called to give me his answer, he said, "Originally, I narrowed the field down to three people. I eliminated one. My final decision was between you and another person. I didn't know who to choose, so I flipped a coin and you lost."

I slammed the phone down and thought maybe I wasn't meant to be an attorney. The doubt was there in a nanosecond. It didn't take long to be unmasked as an imposter. The power of words can be quite significant.

Whether using interoffice email, public email, social media, or a blog, I have been careful with how I use ideas and words. When I needed to convey a harsh thought to another, it was done personally. I would always let the person know that I specifically chose to tell them personally rather than publically. It is critical to keep as many solid and effective relationships as possible. I have witnessed several occasions where a subordinate became a boss to their boss years later.

These experiences demonstrate three key points:
1. Do not underestimate the power of words.
2. Do not be afraid to ask questions.
3. Choose your own distinct communication style and cultivate it.

Are you a flamethrower or a fire extinguisher?
Flamethrower:
You are not careful how you communicate online.

Fire Extinguisher:
Face-to-face communication will provide lasting and fulfilling relationships. Online communication can't accomplish the same thing.

Contemplation Page

Why do you still find it necessary to interrupt others when they are speaking?

....
....
....
....
....

How would you rate yourself as a listener with 1 being the lowest score and 10 being the highest score? What steps can you take today to improve your *listening score*?

....
....
....
....
....

What kind of impact do you believe *Interactive Listening* will have on future conversations?

....
....
....
....
....

CHAPTER 4
REJECT NEGATIVE THOUGHTS

It's not the situation, but whether we react (negative) or respond (positive) to the situation that's important.

ZIG ZIGLAR

LIFE IS BEST LIVED WITH A POSITIVE MINDSET.

Mr. Ziglar said, "Positive thinking won't let you do *anything*, but it will help you do everything better than negative thinking will."

Positive thinkers are sometimes surprised to discover setbacks or obstacles in their path. Accordingly, they must always assess challenges to determine whether they can be overcome. For example, no matter how positive his thinking was, Mr. Zigler could never enter a boxing ring and defeat the heavyweight champion of the world. Nor could he don a surgical mask, remove your appendix and have you survive.

A positive thinker uses a concept I call *objective corrective thinking*. An objective corrective thinker will look at all the facts—including obstacles—and will always ask, "What steps do I need to take to continue my journey?"

Imagine starting up your car. When you insert the key or push the ignition button, the car will start and you can begin your journey. Everything flows from this sequence. Similarly, when you are in a positive frame of mind, you will be able to move in the direction of your choice. On the other hand, if your car won't start, you have a problem and your journey will be delayed. This is what happens when you have negative thoughts. You will be stuck dead in your tracks in a quagmire of non-action.

The Belief Law and the Power of the Mind

When I was young, my dad would take me to the batting cages so I could practice hitting a baseball. The machine would throw one ball after another and I would swing and swing until I made contact.

Our minds are like that machine—throwing out one thought after another—every second of every day. The type of thought that is produced will determine what you will achieve in your lifetime, which is also a direct result of what you believe. For example, if you believe that life is difficult and unfair, I suppose it will be just that.

In fact, there is a law that will always stand the test of time. I named it the Belief Law. It states that what people *believe* to be true is much more important than what is true. A corollary to this law similarly states that nothing has meaning except the meaning that you give it.

Taken together, these laws provide you with tremendous power and ability to decide how to interpret events in your life. After all, you are the author of your life's story, the director of your life's next scene and the creator of your own masterpiece. How you use your mind will determine how things go in your life. Those who let their minds use them are the ones that get stuck in a quagmire. Positive thinking empowers you to believe that the world is yours and that you are a creative force making things happen.

The Rule: You create your own reality. Negative thinking and inappropriate beliefs go hand in hand and can turn you into a victim rather easily. Whenever rational thought is dominated by pure emotion, like a car, you can overheat and wind up going nowhere. On the other hand, your chances of prevailing over a challenge or obstacle increases with objective corrective thinking. Like the car that works, you will arrive at your destination.

Thoughts are very powerful. Discounting and ignoring their affect is a huge mistake. Mr. Ziglar reminds us that a raindrop takes no responsibility for a flood. A snowflake takes no responsibility for a blizzard. Yet, each plays a part. Your thoughts play a huge part how things will turn out. Accomplishments are not limited by birth or skin color but by the size of your hope. More hope means a better future. Less hope means a diminished future.

It is also important to keep in mind that you are a winner in every way. The proof: You were born despite odds of millions to one. One sperm saw one egg and took off in hot pursuit— they connected, and out you came. You were a winner before you were born. You already overcame *incredible odds*. With positive thinking, your success odds are overwhelmingly in your favor. Thoughts are the springboard for *winning ways*. You can remain the winner you already are. It is just a choice that you make.

Problems Are a Good Thing

You may be thinking that making more money, or meeting the right person, or getting the right job, or getting that good grade, would make my life perfect. This wishful thinking is really negative in spirit. There is no such thing as *perfect* and problems never go away on their own. Of course, you can refuse to identify a situation as a problem—

as something that needs attending to. The point is that circumstances and situations are dynamic and forever changing. However, if you remember to be in *Learning mode*, you will see each problem as an opportunity. The choice is rather simple. You can lose (fix) the problem or lose your mind over the problem. Life experiences can provide incredible teaching moments. If you wish for the day that problems would cease, let me remind you that the only folks not facing problems are those residing in cemeteries.

How You See Yourself
Self-esteem defines the reputation you have with yourself. When it is healthy and positive, you can move mountains. When it is anything else it can lead to unhappiness and despair. Think of the times when you believed that you didn't deserve love, happiness, or success. Think of the times when you unconsciously sabotaged desires you didn't believe you should have. There are so many stories of brilliant people sabotaging their careers because of negative thinking and low self-esteem. Perhaps you know someone like this.

In the corporate world, we have seen several executives who "had it all" and ended up losing it to a jail cell. They include Bernie Madoff, the king of the Ponzi schemes, Jeffrey Skilling (Enron), Dennis Kozlowski (Tyco) and Bernie Ebbers (WorldCom).

A peek into politics provides many examples of individuals who sabotaged their careers. Gary Hart and John Edwards saw their presidential hopes shattered when each denied extramarital affairs. Anthony Weiner resigned from Congress and failed in his bid to become mayor of New York City, due to a sexting scandal. Bill Clinton's presidential legacy will be forever tarnished by his conduct in the White House, which led to his impeachment. The list goes on and on.

What about the rest of us? From time to time, we lose our internal compass, which can cause us to act out in more common and nefarious ways. This brief and incomplete list would include passing judgment, making destructive and hurtful comments and speaking while angry, not to mention any type of sexual misbehavior and/or harassment.

Managing Anger
It is crucial to be aware of your feelings. To ignore them until they erupt is like driving through a red light. Very dangerous. Uncontained anger can spread like a wildfire. It ceases only after it has consumed everything in its path. Things said in anger will cause hurt, pain and misery. Once the emotionally laden thought is expressed, the damage has been done. It cannot be taken back. Congratulations, you have hit your intended target. The battle has begun.

It's How You Respond That Counts
Imagine that an inattentive driver has cut you off on the freeway. Your first reaction is to yell and scream—until you notice other drivers looking at you. If you thought that the inattentive driver must have had an emergency, or that you were fortunate you were alert and avoided an accident, or you pity that driver because sooner or later he or she will cause an accident, you have effectively managed your anger. When you tend to personalize every annoying, unpleasant situation as if you were the intended target, you invite anger into the equation.

Whenever you are faced with an issue, sudden or not, do you typically look for one single cause? Does it ever occur to you that there could be another cause? For example, if you automatically blamed the person in the other car for cutting you off on the freeway, did it even occur to you to question whether you were going too fast or too slow?

Let's look at one more thought strategy that can be used to temper anger and negativity. We'll use a sport analogy to get the point across. Imagine that you are a baseball player up at bat. How do you view the pitcher—as an adversary or as someone who could provide you with an opportunity to get a hit? Notice the cataclysmic shift in perception. Notice how you feel more relaxed by viewing the pitcher as being on your side. The pitcher can now serve you opportunities for success.

The stoplight situation is also something you may wish to consider. Before reacting, you will notice the red light in your mind's eye, imploring you to immediately stop what you are doing. This means you will, at worst, delay your reaction to a particular stimulus.

The yellow light means that you will acknowledge your feelings and review alternative responses. The green light signals you to finally respond in the most appropriate manner, considering both the long- and short-term effects of the chosen response.

I remember negotiating with an argumentative lawyer on a complicated real estate matter. Actually, it is more accurate to say we were screaming at each other. Neither one of us heard what the other was saying. The hotter he got, the angrier I got. When I got home that night, I analyzed the day like I did each night. I noted how useless the time had been. Our clients expected us to finish the agreement per their instructions.

The next day, I intended to do that more effectively. As I entered the conference room, the attorney picked up where he had left off. He was yelling and cursing, as he turned red with rage. I didn't take the bait. I got right down to work. I re-crafted fair terms which satisfied each of our clients. He was more interested in displaying his emotions. I was more interested in a fair deal for my client. *Staying calm when another refuses to do so is a winning strategy.*

Likewise, how you think will directly affect how much good comes into your life. Your thoughts are the foundation to your success. As you proceed in this book, you will build upon factors that will prevent you from wounding your self-esteem and will also help you promote *objective corrective thinking* at the appropriate times.

MY STORY

My life was turned upside down on July 20, 1975 with the suddenness of an erupting volcano. The seizure was so violent that it threw me off the bed. In an instant, my bright future disintegrated into thin air.

Black Swan Event #1 had hit. Such an event is an unexpected, devastating occurrence, which has a significant impact on your life. There I was, healthy one day and then deathly ill the next. This was difficult for a 24 year-old to handle, especially when I saw my mind go from *sharp as can be* to *I can't even think.*

I don't remember much about the ambulance ride to Akron-Canton airport, the week I spent in Akron General Hospital, the flight to LaGuardia Airport in New York City or the ambulance ride to Mt. Sinai Hospital.

My mind was a jumbled mess. My mental descent was as quick and severe as a lead pipe plummeting into a body of water. I became my own worst enemy. No hope meant no future. This mental death spiral couldn't be stopped. I was diagnosed with a mass of undetermined origin that was growing in my brain. In 1975, the CAT scan and MRI were not yet developed. While the problem was very serious, two distinct groups of doctors differed on the ultimate diagnosis. One was survivable. The other was not. One platoon of doctors was convinced that I had a malignant brain tumor. The other team believed it was a brain abscess, an infection.

A few days after entering the hospital in Manhattan, I became paralyzed on my left side. The fast-growing mass was exerting tremendous pressure on the surrounding tissue. The intermittent headaches were excruciating.

Prior to the surgery, I remember going into a lecture room with 20 or 30 doctors, seated in rows. I was the subject for their session. After my case was described, I was asked a series of questions. The two I remember were "Spell hospital backwards" and "Count back from 100 by sevens." I couldn't do it. I kept making mistakes. All those eyes staring at me. I felt momentarily that I was back in class at elementary school. That feeling of poor self-esteem came rushing back.

It's amazing how some thoughts have an unlimited shelf life.

In second grade, I was given the dunce cap I would wear for years. In third grade, I still wore the crown. In fourth grade, I was still King of the Dummies. Through the years, I was the last one chosen for spelling bees and show and tell. I was never the blackboard monitor. I stopped volunteering answers because the class collectively laughed at me.

How I wanted to become invisible.

Curse those teachers for not seeing my pain and hurt. I wasn't a person. I had become a label—*that dumb kid.* A label isn't a person. A label is a thing, something that can be kicked around and discarded. A label embodying poor self-esteem does not disappear in a day.

When I needed to spell hospital backwards and count

backwards by 7s, I was lost. In fact, it can take years and in some cases, like mine, decades, for the damage to be completely undone.

The brain surgery was performed on August 11, 1975. My family held their collective breath. When my dad's friend, who had privileges at the hospital, came running into the surgical waiting area, he yelled, "It's an infection." My dad promptly passed out, probably from exhaustion and the joy of hearing the words he had prayed he would someday hear.

Post-surgery, I was on a tremendous amount of anti-convulsive medication which was supposed to prevent further seizures. That was exactly what the medication did not do. I was a mental and physical mess. I lost 30 pounds and was thinking in slow motion. If I weighed 100 pounds upon discharge it was a lot.

When I returned to my room from intensive care, I was in no shape to see what my illness was doing to my wife Shelley and to the rest of the family. Why did they have to suffer, too? At least in front of me, my parents were as strong as the Rock of Gibraltar. Soon, I learned the extent of their suffering. They did a great job of acting. My mom displayed incredible courage. One floor below, my Uncle Howie (my mom's brother) lay dying from lung cancer. I remember I had a bunch of questions about his death and about my illness. Why him? Why so young? Why now? How could one family suffer so much pain at one time? What did I do to deserve this? Why was I being punished? Why did this happen to me? Why me? Why me?

This was a steady refrain. The *why me* question was answered by an unassuming lady. My mother-in-law, Molly - with all the love she could muster - said the most profound words ever spoken to me.

"Dennis, if you didn't say, 'why me' when things were going well in your life, you can't say 'why me' now."

These words hit me at my core and would save my life 40 years later. My mother-in-law's wisdom remains unrivaled. Some hinted that I was chosen because I was strong enough to handle it. If only I was weaker, I would have been spared. Others hinted that I might have deserved what happened because I must have done some bad thing in the past. I never did anything bad. That couldn't be it. Others said that if God wasn't punishing me, then I was being taught a lesson. No, that couldn't be it, either. Or, God was testing my resolve to reclaim my life. No, that could not be the reason.

My family was living through hellish times. Shelley's life was shattered, especially during the uncertain diagnosis period. Our dreams were wiped out. My mother was taken to the edge of sanity by the specter of losing a son and a brother at the same time. God was extracting a mighty price, it seemed.

I tried to understand this illness through the lens of religion. After many years, I have concluded that religion gives us a filter to look at life. I believe that God didn't make me ill for a reason. There is a certain randomness to life. An uncertain future is bearing down on each of us. Uncertainty is the price we pay for being alive. What God does do is give us the strength to cope with a problem. He lets us know that there is a community of people willing to rally around us when we are in need. He reminds us that there may not be a tomorrow and that we need to appreciate our life today. I don't believe in a God who deliberately causes pain in retaliation for a transgression. I believe in a God who constantly reminds us that we are not alone, that our relationships are typically central to how we define ourselves. We just sometimes forget this crucial fact.

Since the brain surgery, I have shared Molly's words with so many people. One day, it suddenly dawned on me that I never told Molly how her words have shaped my life. The next day, I went to visit her. I didn't know whether she would understand. She had advanced dementia and Parkinson's disease. She was unable to effectively communicate. I recounted the story of my brain surgery and hospital stay of many years before. I spoke the words she said to me. I told her that I loved her, thanked her and explained how she had changed my life. I knew she understood, when Gracie, her aide of eight years, wiped the tears from her eyes. Was this another reminder from God? This kind, loving lady passed away three weeks later.

My confidence was snatched from me. Five years after passing the New York State Bar Exam, I finally had the stamina and the confidence to start a law practice. In the meantime, I took an office job in my dad's typesetting shop.

Many years after the surgery, our family was thriving. I wanted to believe that we were destined for smooth sailing. I really didn't believe that we would ever be dealing with Black Swan Event #2. Then I noticed a black and blue mark on my chest. At first, the doctors believed that the lesion occurred when they turned me over on my stomach to perform a discectomy on my back, a surgery for a herniated disc. The mark did not go away. Finally, the dermatologist, after getting the biopsy results, informed me that I had lymphoma. I sat in his office in a state of shock. Not to worry, I was told. It is localized. It just needed to be excised and I would be good as new. The oncologist was also certain about the outcome. He referred me to an oncological surgeon and a plastic surgeon. Everything was under control. The surgery was performed; the cancer was removed and I was one happy fella.

About two months later I was getting pain in my neck and in my sternum. At first, I just thought I had overdone my workout at the gym. The pain would not subside. I consulted with a new oncologist who informed me after additional blood work, bone marrow testing and a PET scan, that I had stage 4 B-cell Lymphoma. I received radiation, chemotherapy and immunotherapy.

During this time, I never asked "Why Me?" Instead, I instinctively knew to say, "Why not me?" This thinking allowed me to maintain a singular focus on getting better and I did. It prevented me from dwelling in a negative world. I *believed* in my doctors and the treatment. I *believed* I would get better. All of that taught me one basic truth.

Nothing has meaning except the meaning that you give it.

Are you a flamethrower or a fire extinguisher?
Flamethrower:
Negative thinking does not let you see the wonderful opportunities and possibilities that are waiting for you.

Fire Extinguisher:
Positive thinking will help you create your own reality.

Contemplation Page

When was the last time that negative thinking prevented you from achieving a goal?

_____
_____
_____
_____
_____

How have *untrue beliefs* affected your life?

_____
_____
_____
_____
_____

What do you think about most of the day? Is it positive or negative?

_____
_____
_____
_____
_____

CHAPTER 5
DEFEND AGAINST ATTITUDE SCLEROSIS

If standard of living is your major objective, quality of life almost never improves, but if quality of life is your number one objective, your standard of living almost always improves.

ZIG ZIGLAR

Negative Thoughts and Attitudes Are Often

a symptom of a mind that has gotten the upper hand. Your mind controls you. You no longer control your mind. Your stinkin thinkin (Mr. Ziglar's term) becomes pervasive. It prevents you from living a healthy, happy, prosperous and secure life with peace of mind and a hopeful future. When such stinkin thinkin festers and continues unchecked, it will have serious consequences. Just for a moment, lets take the stinkin thinkin attitude and treat it as if it were a contagious disease. Just like any serious disease, when its symptoms are ignored, your life will be adversely affected. Let's call this disease Attitude Sclerosis (aka the I/Me disease). Mr. Ziglar referred to the disease as Hardening of the Attitudes.

This affliction overlooks no one. It affects rich and poor, sick and healthy, educated and uneducated. You cannot hide from it because it is so contagious. It reaches everywhere. No matter where you reside or travel, you will discover that Attitude Sclerosis (the I/Me disease) is the leading cause of discord in your personal, family and business life.

It's a Disease

You can conceptualize the effects of the disease by imagining that you are in a room that is completely sealed off. There are no doors or windows. The walls and ceilings are mirrored. Wherever you look, you see a magnified reflection of yourself. Accordingly, your thoughts and views center upon *the self.* Reason, logic and human core values are left behind. As a result, you do not care about the needs or desires of anyone else. Your world has a singular focus: *You.*

Attitude Sclerosis can quickly change a pleasant work environment into a toxic one. The change is complete when a poor work ethic becomes contagious, when company rules are ignored and when lackluster performance, by some, causes colleagues to shoulder additional workloads.

The disease turns life at home upside down too. Yelling becomes the preferred way of communicating and inappropriate behavior becomes the norm inside and outside the home. Promises are never kept.

Recognizing the Symptoms

You will know that you are infected with Attitude Sclerosis when one or more of these symptoms appear:
- You believe that family, friends and co-workers are either with you or against you.
- You develop a self-centered rule-making sense of authority.
- You believe you are entitled to something before you have earned the right to receive it.
- You fail to consider other people's points of view.
- You insist that you are right and everyone else is wrong.
- You create a continuous atmosphere of anxiety.
- You believe that everyone owes you something, i.e., a job, respect, loyalty, love, etc.
- You write off people when they do not agree with you.
- You constantly criticize others and ridicule those who do not follow your directions.
- You always announce how smart you are.
- You say whatever comes into your mind without a filter.
- Your constant refrain is "What's in it for me?"

When these symptoms are ignored and the disease progresses unchecked, you will find yourself alone, without steady employment, unloved and unwanted. Integrity will not exist for you. You will be unable to make effective decisions.

Instructive Suppositions

Here's an example of an *expedient* decision caused by the disease: Suppose the top of your desk is filled with papers. You decide that it is time to clean the surface. You could neatly stack the papers, review them, or file them a way. This takes time and requires major effort. Instead, you sweep the papers onto the floor by moving your arm across the desk. You now have a clean desk. You have also created another issue. All the papers that were once on the desk are now on the floor. This I/Me thinking seems to provide a solution to a problem—but does it, really?

Suppose you are a salesperson attempting to make the biggest sale of your life. The customer hesitates. You panic and plead with the customer. *Make my life easy. I need this sale.*

Imagine you are a doctor, lawyer, accountant, or financial planner. Your client or patient is hanging on to every word you say. You are very busy. It's time to see the next person so you take one last question. Instead of answering, you abruptly end the consultation, leaving your client or patient dazed and confused after you short-changed them.

You are a student who has not worked diligently and are in danger of failing. You plead with your teacher to give you a passing grade. In return, you promise to work harder during the next semester.

Maybe you have been working for the same company for several years and have never given it your all. Currently, the company is quite profitable. Your co-workers have received a raise, you have not. You plead with your boss to give you a raise. You promise to work harder going forward.

Picture your family gathered together for the holidays. A parent refuses to speak with an adult child or an adult child refuses to speak with a parent because something hurtful was said many years ago. This is a manifestation of the disease in its extreme form.

In the salesperson example, you have antagonized the only person that can put money in your pocket. In the professional example, you failed to be concerned about the needs and fears of the client or patient, insuring that referrals will not be made. In the student example, you must *learn* before you can *earn* the grade. The employee example shows that you must deserve the boss's praise before you can get a raise. The family example brings home the point that the disease prevents you from realizing that you could be the one at fault. When you say, "It's your fault, not mine," you have alleviated the need to examine your own actions. Maybe *it's my fault* will sadly never enter your mind. Congratulations, you have antagonized the person you seek love from the most. Think of your family right now. When was the last time you told your spouse or significant other that you love him or her? What about your children or your parents?

These examples illustrate how people sell themselves short to the one person who has the power—through a referral, grade, job, or love—to significantly affect their lives.

The Cure

The cure is rather simple. It requires that you satisfy the needs of others before you satisfy your own. Attitude Sclerosis causes you to do the opposite. This multi-step plan requires that you take vital steps. In fact, your life will be more rewarding when you do as many of the following "cures" as possible:

- Behold the universal truth: *You get by giving.* Burn this into your mind and hold it close to your heart.
- Listen more than you speak. Listen with the intent to understand, not to respond.
- Acknowledge the other person's point of view.
- End all relationships amicably and never burn any bridges.
- Refrain from reacting emotionally. Like the sports team that needs to gain its composure, take a time-out. Don't lose sight of the ultimate prize (job, relationship, etc.).
- Set a goal of saying nothing *negative* about other people.
- Take the initiative to maintain peace and calm in your environment.
- Sincerely praise your friends, colleagues and family members. There is no better medicine known to man than sincere praise.
- Concentrate on the things you can control, like your thoughts and feelings. You cannot control someone else's actions, behavior, or feelings.
- Don't retaliate or seek revenge.
- Avoid sarcastic comments.
- Begin each day with the belief that you will help someone in need.
- Talk back to the negative voices in your head. Show them who is in control.

Here is a compelling reason to consider one or more of these cures:

Nothing changes if nothing changes.

The Power to Choose Your Behavior
So far, you have considered the kind of person you are and the kind of person you wish to become. You have been given the key to unlock the door to a good life. Take the key. Put it in the lock and turn it. Welcome! You have just opened the door to your exciting future. Breathe in the deep wisdom that you have just acquired. In time, you will become a better friend, lover, relative, colleague and business associate. You will realize that mutual relationships exist when you are there for the other person. Kindness to yourself and to others can overcome your old default pattern to strike back.

There is a veritable library of how to say the same thing in a different, less caustic and antagonistic way. Why not express the same thing with grace? It will get you further. You won't live in a world where favors are traded or counted. Rather, favors are done simply because you want to do them. And best of all, when you do them, you will feel better about yourself. When your horizons are broader and larger than yourself, like a controlled fire, you will absorb its power and heat and provide warmth to others in need. Kindness provides you with persuasive power.

While it is true that you can't always choose your feelings at a given moment, you can choose how you will behave. Zig Ziglar articulated one of life's universal truths: "You can have everything in life you want, if you just help enough other people get what they want."

MY STORY
My father-in-law Jack was a humble, kind and caring man. After he passed, as I was cleaning out his desk drawers, I found a folder filled with thank you letters from people he had helped through the years. He had lived the universal truth—that you get by giving. Dad gave and he never talked about his acts of unvarnished kindness. I'll never forget that.

I loved law school. It teaches you how to think. In public school, my mind was my greatest deficit. In law school, my mind was my greatest asset. Yet, there was a voice lurking in the back of my mind that I could not quiet.

If you go to law school, you should want to be a lawyer. I didn't know that I wanted to be a lawyer. After all, there was the family business. The "easy" route was rearing its ugly head again. When my peers would talk about the kind of law they wanted to practice, there was passion and conviction behind their words. I was jealous. But I had a family business to take over, or so I thought. I was totally wrong. It would belong to my brother because he earned the right, whereas I just wanted it. Little did I know it would be the business that almost destroyed any modicum of self-respect that remained. (More on that later.)

Over the years, I have gotten better at reigning in emotional outbursts. I believe that a lot of this issue had to do with my years of self-imposed invisibility when I was very young, when my thoughts, ideas and beliefs didn't matter to my teachers and some classmates.

It took many years to part ways with these thoughts. When I felt ignored, I would fight for my visibility. Today, I concentrate on my choices and my attitude in each life situation. How I act, how I behave and how I respond are my purposeful choices.

Just the other day, I was waiting to pull into a space at a shopping center. A car pulled into that space as I waited for the car pulling out to pass me. A fury momentarily exploded inside me, which would have normally caused an outward, explosive reaction. I was upset and yet I caught myself and let the feeling subside.

To evolve to a point where I'm aware of my choices and attitude is a precious gift. I feel as if I'm living for a second time. This is what can happen when you apply the lessons learned from living life, just as I was happy to learn again from my father-in-law after he sadly passed.

Are you a flamethrower or a fire extinguisher?
Flamethrower:
By the time you realize you are infected by this disease, a lot of damage will have been done. Relationships with others will have been compromised, at home and on the job.

Fire Extinguisher:
When you change for the better, the results can be staggering. By focusing on the needs of others, you will be helping yourself achieve more as well.

Contemplation Page

Would you say that your various relationships at home and at work are flourishing or are in trouble? In either case, why is that so?

How many of the symptoms in our symptom list apply to you?

How many of the cures have you tried and how effective have you found them to be?

CHAPTER 6

STOP WASTING TIME AND PUT YOUR THOUGHTS INTO ACTION

*If we don't start,
it's certain we can't arrive*
Zig Ziglar

YOUR ANSWERS TO THESE TWO IMPORTANT

questions will determine whether your approach to life will lead to joy, happiness, peace of mind, prosperity and a hopeful future. Consider the following: Are you spending your life chasing and seeking things that are really not important? Are you still on a journey to nowhere with your confused self?

Along the highways and byways of life, you may have found a spouse, family, job, friends and perhaps some wealth. You may appear happy, but be anything but that. Perhaps love in the home is scarce and respect at work is even more so. Perhaps you are merely tolerated by relatives, friends, colleagues and employees. You may finally arrive at a destination only to discover that it is a place you never wished to visit. Too much precious time has gone by and too much energy has been wasted.

You Can't Live Forever

If you had no *expiration date*, wasting time wouldn't be so bad. But, since you will not live forever, it is regrettable not to have used your allotted time wisely. One day, tomorrow will never come. To optimize your accomplishments and joy, you must take your life off autopilot. Mr. Ziglar stresses that you will take action when you finally discover urgency in your life. His point though, is that urgency should always be front and center. It is your life. Get the most out of it. ***Live your story.***

Are you living your story? I hope so. Here's the thing to keep in mind: You can live your life anyway that you choose, BUT you get to do it only once. What would you do differently if you had *just one chance to make things right?* Think how your behavior would change toward those you respect and love.

Tick . . . tick . . . tick . . .

The clock of life never stops ticking. You need to take stock of your life *now*. It is time to learn from your problems and embrace your challenges, while you persevere through individual predicaments and escape from the past.

Tick . . . tick . . . tick . . .

It is time to set your sites on new horizons. Bob Beaudine, in his book, *The Power of Who*, says, "If you want to have something you've never had before, you've got to be willing to do something that you've never done before."

The time is now to capture that distant dream. You may be thinking that it's too late or that you are too old. No! Hundreds of people have created a second act later in life. There is a difference between being busy and being effective. Stop being like the octopus on roller skates.

Tick . . . tick . . . tick . . .

Are you one who believes that life is like a nine-inning baseball game or a 60-minute football game, that there is a specific time to call it quits? I have a surprise for you. The game of life is more like a game board. It is *your* life. It is *your* game board. This means that *you* determine whether and when to respond, react, or do nothing. If you are not convinced to keep moving forward, here is another question: What if you decided to give up on yourself and then saw someone in your exact position turn things around-how would you feel?

Tick . . . tick . . . tick . . .

Here is one final thought to keep in mind: Life is meant to be hard. Adversity will provide you with the opportunity to stretch yourself out of your comfort zone. Life would be boring and unsatisfying if it were like a magical golf club, where every swing puts the ball in the cup. Soon you would tire from swinging this magical club. It would bring no joy. There would be no challenge. You would stop playing. If life mirrored our magical golf club, there would be no reason to try to stretch your abilities and reach the next plateau. There would be no reason to get up in the morning. But thankfully, there is. Life is a test and the challenge is to be the *best you* possible, which will allow you to celebrate with gratitude a life well-lived. Happiness could be just around the corner.

Tick . . . tick . . . tick . . .

Nature's Law
This concept is critical to remember as it connects the future directly to what is done in the present. Nature's law requires that you plant seeds *today* to reap a harvest *tomorrow*. For example, the seed of

friendship planted today can blossom into a feast of love tomorrow. The seed of ideas and hard work sown today can grow into the fruit of solutions and a career tomorrow. There are no shortcuts, quick fixes, or super-quick routes to achieving goals. The process is like the workings of an old typewriter—achieved one steady keystroke at a time.

Sustained triumphs of a lifetime require changing your mindset from short-term gratification to a longer, more strategic view. This is not easy, especially in today's world of instant gratification and it is understandable why so many people believe in instant results.

Speedy, super-quick and super-fast seems to be the natural pace and rhythm of life today. Products purchased online can be delivered the same day. Thoughts and opinions circulate the globe in a blink of an eye. Prodigious processing capacity allows products to communicate with each other. Because significant change is ubiquitous, it is no surprise that you feel overwhelmed and sometimes feel that you just can't keep up with the latest developments.

The exponential rise in computer processing power has enabled unimaginable changes in a relatively short period of time. In our hyper-connected world, it has been estimated that this century alone will see the equivalent of 20,000 years of progress. Accordingly, folks expect similar results in their family, personal and business lives—speedy, super-quick and super-fast. Some of us remember that typewriters were around for over 100 years before they were replaced by word processors.

So Much Is Possible

President Kennedy, when speaking about the then-incipient space program in the early 1960s, underscored the need for action. He felt it was important to explore space—not because it was easy, but because it was hard. JFK knew that the easiest thing to do was nothing at all. During this time, one phrase in particular became quite popular whenever someone thought that you couldn't accomplish something. In that moment, they would say, "You could no more do that than put a man on the moon."

Luckily, President Kennedy didn't listen. He knew that *decision time* galvanizes creative and imaginative forces that can overcome most any obstacle. Since the United States put a man on the moon, this phrase now stands for the proposition that so many things are possible. In fact, people now say, "If we can put a man on the moon we can do anything." And, why not?

This reaction should become yours, too. In fact, asking "Why not?" requires that you ACT NOW.

ACT stands for **A C**hampion **T**omorrow. If you want to be a champion to yourself, your family and friends, your colleagues and your boss, you must ACT and do it now. This means that you can no longer afford to delay making decisions when the time is ripe. The act does not have to contain a forward motion. But, it does need to be part of a thought out strategy. Sometimes, staying put, moving sideways or even backwards may be the best gambit to advance your goal.

NOW stands for **N**ew **O**pportunity **W**aits. Nature's law rewards those who are planting those seeds. **N**ew **O**pportunities will always **W**ait for those who have done the preparation and the planning.

A Dream

Imagine freezing winter weather turning a dark, unlit mountain highway into a slick surface of invisible ice. As your car comes out of a turn, it suddenly spins out of control. You frantically pump the brakes, but your car continues its directionless, solitary journey over a seemingly endless stretch of frozen water. Your panic and fruitless efforts to regain control exacerbate the unrelenting and uncontrollable slide until your car catapults over a steep embankment.

As you are about to open death's door, you wake up, avoiding a fatal result.

This horrible dream appears as your "sub-par" year is about to come to a merciful end. It re-appears at the start of every New Year, as a reminder to do better, which prompts you to make another set of meaningless promises—the same ones you make to yourself each year.

"Next year will be different!" You tell yourself that, "It will be a year of accomplishment, full of successes."

However, as you tabulate the results in your career and personal life, you sadly realize that "next year" is simply a sad refrain of the unspectacular previous years. This dream is reminding you that once again you have failed to take control of your life.

The big question is how to regain control and direction over your life so you can reverse this cycle and make next year your year.

Take Action Today, Become A Champion Tomorrow
Tom Dempsey played in the National Football League for 11 years. For quite some time, he held the record for kicking the NFL's longest field goal. He would never have accomplished this feat if he had listened to the opinions of those who said that a player without toes on his kicking foot and without fingers on his right hand could never be a kicker in the NFL.

Jim Abbott pitched in the Major Leagues for ten years, including a no-hitter while with the New York Yankees. That is amazing—the stuff of fairytales. But he would never have accomplished this feat if he had listened to the opinions of others who said that a pitcher with one functional arm could never pitch in professional baseball by throwing and catching a baseball with the same arm and hand.

I admire both of these men. While growing up, each learned that everything was possible. They believed in Nature's Law, understood the power of the mind, never became a prisoner to their condition and understood that there is no substitute for positive thought—teamed with action, planning and preparation. Tom and Jim, each in their own way, became **A Champion Tomorrow**.

Their stories remind us to make this year our year. You can too, by taking action and believing in yourself. Don't let some dream-robber snatch your dreams from you. When you **ACT NOW** you can change your life. After all, if we can put a man on the moon why can't you reach your goals, too?

MY STORY
After brain surgery, I remained in the hospital for three weeks undergoing penicillin therapy. Miraculously, I was back in law school six months later. I believed that surviving the surgery meant that I

was here on this earth to accomplish something special. I told anyone who would listen that this is what I truly believed. I didn't quite know what that special thing would be.

This feeling never left me. Sometimes it was close by, while at other moments it languished. But this idea fueled me with the desire to move forward and complete my legal education.

Truth be told, I was nervous with law school looming a few months away. I was starting to believe that if I could overcome all that I had already faced, I would do fine completing school. I have to admit, walking on to the campus of Hofstra Law School, where I earned the credits I needed to graduate from Akron, started the juices flowing gain. While recuperating I had so much time to think about things. Sometimes that can be dangerous, because you can talk yourself out of the very thing you set out to do. I wanted to be a lawyer. (In retrospect, it would be more accurate to say my parents wanted me to be a lawyer).

My plan was to take the final 18 credits over two semesters because there was still a big question mark regarding my stamina and my ability to concentrate in class each day and keep up with the work.

Things worked out fine. I worked to the limits of my compromised capabilities. Although I felt that I was running a 100-yard dash with weights around my ankles, I finished all the course work within that period and reached my goal. For many years, I told people that to that date, my greatest accomplishment was passing the bar and finishing law school.

Sometimes I marvel over how far I have come. I have learned that my personal journey, no matter how determined I was, was never linear. There were always some steps forward accompanied by an unequal number of steps backwards.

I sometimes grew restless when I couldn't clarify my purpose in life. I had looked in law…and in mortgages…and in business. The search was exhausting. It also took me forever to believe I was entitled to good things in life. Marrying my high school sweetheart was the one thing God grudgingly gave me. I have often said that although I was born in 1951, my life started in 1968 when I saw Shelley by her locker at Roslyn High School.

I had realized that the answer to my purpose in life was

always close by because it was residing within me. The purpose-led life is made up of choices that only comes from an internal place.

Now I get it. I was looking in the wrong places. So as I prepare for my second act, I know exactly what I will do with the remaining time that I have. Do *you* know what you will do?

Are you a flamethrower or a fire extinguisher?
Flamethrower:
You desire everything to be done speedily, super quick and super-fast. This overwhelming need to look for short cuts is a result of a lack of self-discipline. Accordingly, your thought is accompanied by another thought: figuring out a short cut. You do not set priorities because you believe you have all the time in the world to make your mark. What you fail to realize is that one day tomorrow will not come.

Fire Extinguisher:
Nature's Law provides that first and foremost you must work hard to earn the right to achieve, rather than demand something happen now, today, at this very moment. Your thought is accompanied by an act. You know what needs to be done. All that is left is to act. There is always an expiration date to achieve. Dreams will become reality when you have a plan, the grit to achieve it and a target date.

Contemplation Page

What actions will you take to become a *champion of life?*

_____
_____
_____
_____
_____

What will you do now when people tell you that "what you proposed simply can't be done?" How will you respond differently?

_____
_____
_____
_____
_____

What are you going to do to prevent this year from turning into a disappointing year?

_____
_____
_____
_____
_____

CHAPTER 7
KNOW HOW TO PLAN

Lack of direction, not lack of time is the problem. We all have 24 hour days.

ZIG ZIGLAR

A BURNING DESIRE TO ACHIEVE A BETTER LIFE

for yourself and your family is a critical first step. Dreaming about and wishing for a new reality is simply not enough. Preparation and planning will help. This is the basis of Zig & Tom Ziglar's book, *Born to Win*. Your dream will remain an aspiration until you can memorialize it on paper. This takes determination. But, once it is written down and you do the necessary work, the goal can be achieved. You can then add this written down goal to your victory list because it does take courage to start and additional courage not to give up. Good planning also requires the ability to change course when your original assumptions prove faulty.

According to Clayton Christensen, James Allworth and Karen Dillion, authors of the book, *How Will You Measure Your Life?*, switching from a primary strategy (deliberate strategy) to a secondary strategy (emergent strategy) depends on acknowledging additional facts and possibilities. Assumptions must be reality tested. This is accomplished by asking this very important question: What assumptions (facts) would have to be true for this plan to work?

It is best to plan for something difficult when it is easy. By thinking and acting in advance, you can accomplish the most. If you have a habit of postponing action on a task because the plan is not perfect, you could be hurting your chances for success. While you may take pride in acknowledging your perfectionist tendencies, it may be your way of protecting yourself against failure. You can reach a level of "excellence" without being a perfectionist. When you delay action, you could miss the most favorable time to conclude the matter at hand.

Setting Goals

Some people refuse to set goals because they are afraid of not reaching them. So, they think it's better not set any at all. Others don't set goals because they just don't know how. Others refuse to set goals because of a poor self-image. The other reason people don't set goals is because they have never been sold on the idea. Now that you have gotten this far in your reading, there is no reason not to set your goals down on paper.

Mr. Ziglar created a detailed, logical process for planning goals, which consists of seven sequential steps and is used by thousands of people throughout the world. While the list is short, it requires thoughtful planning and preparation.
1. Determine your goal. Have a specific target. After all, you can't hit a target you do not have.
2. List the benefits you will receive when you reach that goal.
3. Note the obstacles you will have to overcome.
4. List the skills and knowledge you will need to make your goal attainable.
5. List the people and groups who can help you.
6. Develop a plan of action.
7. Set an achievement date.

Planning, Nurturing, Persistence and Timing
Are you still afraid of giving a sustained effort? It's understandable that trying hard and failing to achieve your desired result could be devastating to your psyche. Today, the added pressure to succeed is rather severe. If you don't achieve a result, you may be considered a failure. Your friends, boss or even your family can be quick to assign negative labels.

In the eighteenth century, if you failed at achieving your goal, you were said to have "made a failure." Since life is a perpetual classroom, failure and adversity should always be welcomed. Your job is to convert the mistake of yesterday into the success of tomorrow.

Preparation and planning require a laser-like focus. It is often a good idea to truncate a plan into smaller pieces because you will advance further by taking steady, small steps instead of taking one giant leap.

Planning acts essentially as fertilizer. An idea, like a seed that is planted, needs a proper environment and time to germinate. With that in mind, it is equally important to recognize that things will not happen merely because you want them to. There is always a gestation period. Things happen at the right time because there is a coalescence of forces and the pieces have fallen into place. The same holds true for your ideas and goals. They need a symbiosis of planning, nurturing and persistence. They will happen, perhaps not at the exact time you want them to happen, but they will eventually happen. People who employ a process understand this. People who are merely outcome-focused will never understand.

An outcome is dependent on many factors beside your input. That is why many people who are outcome-focused often get thrown for a loop and give up when they do not achieve their desired result. But, when you are process-focused, you work diligently at improving your personal and mental skills, even if it doesn't result in the desired outcome.

You keep at it. Eventually you will get the outcome you desire. A great friend of planning is persistence. It is shortsighted to believe that you must succeed on your first attempt or it's not worth it. Quitting or giving up is a permanent solution to a temporary problem. The choice of how to proceed is always yours.

As Zig Ziglar always said, "You were born to win, but to be the winner you were born to be, you must plan to win and prepare to win. Then and only then, can you legitimately expect to win."

Now you know how.

MY STORY

A lack of planning has significantly impacted my life. Since I was a little boy, I always wanted to be a doctor. That was all I talked about. It was my biggest desire. My mother would always bring animal organs home from the butcher. I would promptly dissect the hearts, livers and spleens. You name it; I examined it.

I always felt medicine was my calling. When I started at Adelphi University, I took the toe-in-the-water approach to committing to *Pre-Med* as a major. *Let's see how I do in biology,* I thought. Not only did I get an "A" in the course; the biology professor wanted to take me under his wing. He strongly urged me to commit to the pre-med program.

What would you do if a well-respected professor expressed interest in being your mentor? Would you take advantage of this opportunity? Of course, you would. I remained neutral. Next, I took chemistry over the summer with a professor who was an incredibly hard marker. I received a grade of "B". I was thrilled with this grade, but still I would not commit. I then decided to enroll in Organic Chemistry, the hardest course in the *Pre-Med* curriculum, where I did quite poorly. My lab work was sloppy and inadequate at best and the coursework threw me for a loop. I dropped the course. Not committing to the *Pre-Med* program insured my failure. I met my self-fulfilling prophecy. My unsteady confidence and lack of self-esteem brought me back to second grade.

My parents couldn't proclaim, "My son, the doctor" but there was always, "My son, the lawyer." I flourished in the *Pre-Law* program, acing courses in business, constitutional law and labor law. My brother, Bruce, was already enrolled at Case Western Reserve Law School. "My sons, the lawyers" was even better.

After practicing law for 18 years, I decided to leave the field. Being a lawyer was not who I was. I realized it was not my dream. I climbed the ladder of success only to discover it was leaning against the wrong building.

This is where planning comes into play. Life contains obstacles. They have to be met head-on. In college, the only plan I came up with—because it represented the path of least resistance—was to cut my losses and run. Forget medicine. Embrace law. What I did not consider at the time were other reasonable options.

I could have obtained extra help from the professor.

I could have hired a teaching assistant as a tutor.

If those two options did not pan out, I could have taken the course again. But, I didn't.

When you're young, it is so easy to convince yourself that the alternative option you have chosen is the correct one. Quick fixes and easy gains have their appeal. But their long-term effectiveness is very limited.

Are you a flamethrower or a fire extinguisher?
Flamethrower:
Quitting is a permanent solution to a temporary problem.

Fire Extinguisher
Should the plan be unsuccessful, say, "I *made* a failure," instead of "I *am* a failure."

Contemplation Page

If your perfectionist attitude is preventing you from fulfilling your dreams, what steps are you taking to change the situation?

....
....
....
....
....

What can you do to become more effective and efficient in the way you plan?

....
....
....
....
....

What skills need to be acquired, updated and/or improved upon?

....
....
....
....
....

CHAPTER 8

OPTIMIZE YOUR IMPORTANT RELATIONSHIPS

Some people find fault like there is a reward in it.

Zig Ziglar

RELATIONSHIPS PROVIDE THE NECESSARY SEEDS

for growth. Durable relationships are built on trust, caring and respect. You can either untie a relationship or solidify it by uniting with the other person. The only difference between the two words is the placement of the letter "I". Its placement is critical. When you care about the "I" primarily or exclusively, you'll untie the relationship by forsaking the needs of the other person. However, when you consider that person equally, you can unite with them. When this happens the "I" becomes a "We", allowing the relationship to flourish. Successful relationships depend upon a reciprocal nurturing, caring and valuing of all individuals. An association becomes a catalyst for great achievements when the underlying support and encouragement is meaningful and sincere.

Attitude Sclerosis, discussed in Chapter 5, causes relationships to disintegrate. Real fulfillment in life never occurs at the expense of another. Rather, it manifests itself when you become somebody's somebody. Because everyone's humanity is bound together—it is indivisible and service to one is service to all. But, those who are afflicted with the disease, will find a reason to knock you down; rattle you; and intimidate you. Should you catch it, you will do the same thing to people in your sphere of influence. Until you are cured, your life will never be about helping another. It will be about defeating them.

A person walking around with the disease will also become petty, disoriented and angry. Their pernicious beliefs about life, as noted in the *symptom list,* creates problems wherever they go. Such a person would do well to remember the tale of Captain Ahab in *Moby Dick.* He is consumed by anger and harbors a thirst for revenge. His only desire is to kill the whale that chewed off his leg. When he finally sees the whale, he gets caught in the rope of the harpoon and is thrown into the water and drowns. This ageless story teaches that unchecked anger will ultimately destroy. When you go it alone, the stories you tell yourself lack the caring feedback from others. There will usually be a difference between *the event* and *your perception* of that event. If the captain had heard from others, perhaps he could have seen that he was lucky to be alive and that there was plenty left for him to accomplish.

Attitude Sclerosis also forces you to keep score. Life becomes a continuous mathematical equation, which will always be out of balance. *I did this for you, so now it's your turn to do this for me.* Score keeping is anathema to those who care about maintaining personal, business and family relationships.

The Most Difficult Relationship
Much has been written about honoring parents. The Ten Commandments says, "Honor thy father and thy mother." Much less has been written about mothers and fathers honoring their children. The relationship between child and parent is probably the most complicated of all. It is the job of a parent to make their children happy and healthy individuals who can persevere through periods of uncertainty. This requires that the child have foundational skills in problem solving and dealing with stressful situations. Additionally, the child must be able to develop any needed skills along the way.

Sometimes, a child provides the opportunity for a parent to have a "do over." You may have wanted to excel in some endeavor, such as athletics, but didn't. Now, you'll make sure that your child will make that dream come true by proxy. But, if you expect your child to sacrifice their dreams to make you happy, you are cheating your child out of living their life. Once the child is old enough to realize what has happened, your relationship will suffer. Everyone gets to live life only once. You had your chance. Give your children theirs.

When children are young, it is so important that they see their parents make mistakes. And it is important for the child to see that their parents can learn from their mistakes. It is likewise vital for children to hear a parent say, "I'm Sorry." Children will never be perfect. Their parents will never be perfect. Yet, each of us are awesome human beings who happen to be flawed. So, let's just say we are *Flawsome* people who strive to be better.

Be that as it may, many parents try to be *perfect,* believing that all they do is in the best interest of their children. You will never get perfect right. Marian Wright Edelman, in her iconic work, *The Measure of our Success: A Letter to My Children and Yours,* says it best in the following quote: "But it is important for us overly perfectionist parents to make clear that you are far more than your SATs, good grades and trophies. However desirable these achievements are and however proud we are of them, they have no bearing on your intrinsic value or on our love for and acceptance of you as a person. No awards can ever rival the countless little and big joys you have given and continue to give to us.

"I seek your forgiveness for all the times I talked when I should have listened; got angry when I should have been patient; acted when I should have waited; feared when I should have delighted; scolded when I should have encouraged; criticized when I should have complimented; said no when I should have said yes and said yes when I should have said no. I did not know a whole lot about parenting or how to ask for help. I often tried too hard and wanted and demanded so much and mistakenly sometimes tried to mold you into my image of what I wanted you to be rather than discovering and nourishing you as you emerged and grew..."

Slipping up on your parental duties is okay, providing you use the principle we discussed earlier. It is important that any mistake be corrected quickly.

Stop saying, *"If only I..."* This phrase signifies that you are resigned to your mistake. You are stuck. When it comes to family, you have to elevate your skills. You can do this by saying, *"Next Time I Will..."* In that case, hope is what you need and you just gave it to yourself and your children by adjusting your mindset and your choice of words. You will do better this way and your children will notice and be extremely grateful.

Railroad Thinking

This type of thinking comes into play whenever one person maintains undue influence over another. For example, imagine taking an express train in the wrong direction. Just as you leave the first station, you realize you must take the train to the end of the line before taking it all the way back to that first station. This is a long, time-consuming process.

When children are not permitted to think for themselves, the situation will take a long time to fix. The perfect example of railroad thinking occurs when parents exerts too much influence over their children and refuse to give them wings to fly. The children will end up missing destinations and opportunities because they cannot make decisions on their own.

While the job of a parent is to make sure that their children have the confidence to tackle problems and build meaningful relationships, this is not always the case. Sometimes, older children are quick to give their power away to their parents. They don't realize that their mind is theirs to nurture. Parental control works when the child is young. It does not work when the child needs independence to grow and make independent decisions. Overcoming mistakes and bad decisions spur growth and confidence. Children will not learn from their mistakes if they are not given the opportunity to think for themselves and work through these challenges.

Creating an excessively dependent child who is not capable of navigating through life on his or her own will have dreadful consequences, especially when it comes to choosing jobs and maintaining relationships. When overly dependent children see their close friends sail through life they will become quite frustrated. Eventually, the strain on the parental relationship will minimize mutual trust. As the child struggles for equilibrium and direction, the parent will lay blame on the child for his or her stagnation and the child will blame the parent. These recriminations will waste a lot of time and prevent necessary healing to occur. Mishandling relationships within the family is the biggest mistake you can make.

Defining Character

Character is how you see yourself. Mr. Ziglar taught us that our thoughts become words. Our words become action. Our actions become habits. Our habits become character and our character becomes destiny. Billy Graham believed that character makes up our north star. He also hit on a fundamental truth when he said, "When wealth is lost, nothing is lost; when health is lost, something is lost; when character is lost, all is lost."

Your character will have a significant impact on each of your significant relationships. Therefore, it is important to understand your own character assessment. Ask for feedback from your family and colleagues. You will need to choose someone who is objective and will tell you the truth. When you get their feedback, do not argue. Just say *thank you*. It is possible that you will not like what you hear. Keep in mind that you may not be aware of what may be all too familiar to others.

This exercise could be a real eye-opener. It may surprise you to discover that others, even in your family, view you differently than how you view yourself. Facebook and Twitter often provide a distorted view with "friends" and "likes." What is missing from this mix is deeper context and nuance.

If you find asking for feedback too intimidating, then simply listen to the random remarks colleagues, friends and family make about you every day. Listen for the good, the bad and the ugly. Do this at work and at home and do not defend any negative criticism. Your only job is to listen and make a list for yourself. No one needs to know that you are doing this.

MY STORY

The one spotlight I want shinning on my life resume is GREAT FATHER. I knew Shelley would be a great mom—and she is. I learned from my mom and dad that love is spelled t-i-m-e. They made sure they had plenty for us. We made sure we had plenty for our kids, as well. Our job description required that we assist our children to become happy and healthy individuals, who respect others, are responsible for their actions, and have the ability to make impactful decisions about their lives. Thank goodness we got the only real important thing right. In fact, this is the only real success that counts.

Shelley and I are close to our boys today because we put in the effort and made wise decisions when they were young. Instead of condemning, we always encouraged. We praised their efforts instead of criticizing them or their faults. We tried to create a passion for learning in school and after their formal schooling ended. We wanted them to learn the incredible power of persistency. Accomplishments are not an easy thing to achieve. We wanted them to always dream of things they wanted to do and then do them.

Time goes by fast. In the blink of an eye, children become

adults. And before you know it, they have their own family. As a parent, you hope that you have laid the groundwork for them to achieve success in their personal, family and business lives.

Before their individual careers took off, Jason and Cory worked on various projects together. It brought great joy to see them working and learning together. Their prodigious talents pioneered the bundling of news, information and education on an interactive political news platform—they organized an online community which merged citizen reporting in various conflict zones around the world with traditional journalism— they marketed recyclable bags before that was in vogue—they built a virtual reality broadcasting app. The boys also founded the first real estate brokerage company in Manhattan that incorporated social entrepreneurship into its business plan. The company, through its generous donations to **charity:water**, built several fresh water wells, which finally gave impoverished communities in Africa access to clean drinking water. These accomplishments were vast . Each started with a thought then an act. The boys understand that success comes overtime. It never happens overnight. Mr. Ziglar believed that when you are hard on yourself, life is easy. When you are easy on yourself, life is hard. We are proud of them for who they are. Each possesses the foundation stones of honesty, character, faith, integrity, love and loyalty.

Understanding Different Roles

As their dad, and as an investor and principal of each company, it was sometimes challenging merging the personal side with the business side. While I thoroughly enjoyed watching them work together, I preferred the role of father to any other. I learned during this time, that the best thing that I could do was to let them spread their proverbial wings and fly. The boys understood that different roads could lead to the same place. There is never only one right move. Accordingly, there was always room for another way—an alternative approach. This in my opinion, was one of the biggest lessons that they learned.

A second epiphany: I've seen fathers (and mothers) react negatively when a child offers advice of any kind. I believe that a father becomes a man when he can accept advice (business and personal) from his children. I remember the time I objected to leasing a store-front for our real estate brokerage company – due to financial considerations. The boys were in favor of this strategic move. Ultimately, the company entered into the lease and it turned out to be a sound business decision.

A child needs a parent to offer encouragement, especially when they are young. I remember two sports-related incidents. When Jason was beginning to play organized baseball, I was surprised to discover that he could only throw a baseball a few yards. He had a faulty picture in his mind of what a throw should look like. We practiced every day. First, there was slight improvement. Occasionally, he would zip one in. He knew from our talks that if he did it once, he could do it again. A few weeks into the season, he was throwing the ball as well as any player on the team.

Other children didn't have much of a chance to improve. Parents would yell to their kids, "Can't you catch a ball?" or "If you strike out again, find another ride home." Sad but true. Imagine how children feel hearing such talk from the person who should have been their biggest fan. Yet this behavior, to some degree, invariably happens whenever a child is on a sports team. One can only imagine what happens in the household when that same child brings home a bad grade or one deemed not good enough. Do you think the parent is saying, "You can do better; how can I help?"

Cory loved to pitch. If he gave up a hit, he got mad at himself. If he walked a batter, he got mad at himself. If he gave up a run, he got mad at himself. If he lost a game, he got mad at himself. It took him a while to see that instead of getting mad at yourself, it was important to look at these situations as challenges and to practice harder and attempt to do better next time. Every game became a learning experience. He discovered that it was important to praise the effort of your teammates. The harder you pull for them, the harder they will try for you.

This is true in business as well. Unfortunately, too many forget this principle. Support is something that is earned. So when the shortstop makes an error, you yell out, "Nice try. You'll get the next one!"

Shelley and I always felt that it was important to attend every game. Whether it was baseball, soccer, or basketball, we were there, rooting them on. If each child had a game at the same time, Shelley and I would split up. Our children always had a rooting gallery. It broke my heart to watch parents drop off their child, only to return when the game was over. If you do not do these important things when your children are young, you will lose them as they grow older.

One day, Cory came home from school and asked, "How come you never punish me?"
He continued talking about his friends who get punished all the time. We told him that from now on, he would be punished whenever he did something we didn't like. He walked away with a smile on his face.

Our children understood the importance of taking responsibility for their actions. It started at an early age. They knew that if they misbehaved in school or if they did not do their homework, mommy and daddy would not come to their rescue. They and they alone, would face the consequences. This is a significant lesson to internalize. Instead of circumventing a problem, they learned to meet them head on. Being responsible is the only way to power through life's hurdles and hardships. The earlier children learn this lesson, the better prepared they will be to face an uncertain world full of surprises. They have wonderful, loving and caring spouses and are raising happy children. Each family is establishing their own positive culture where the children understand that *in our family this is how we do things*. The families are supported by the foundation stones mentioned earlier.

Railroad Thinking, Reprised

When I was young, I fell victim to railroad thinking. Although I was accepted to American University, George Washington University, and the University of Hartford, I chose to attend Adelphi University. My brother went there and I knew that he would pave the way for me. He introduced me to his professors, his friends and some fraternity brothers. Going to Adelphi would be easy, I thought. That's it in a nutshell. In the short-term, taking the path of least resistance will always have the potential to take you for an unwanted ride.

You need resistance to build character. You need to stand on your own two feet—be independent. Most of all, you need to make your own decisions. This holds true even if you wind up making a wrong decision.

I went to Adelphi for all the wrong reasons. I received a first-rate education but it was not a truly independent decision. My parents influenced me, as they wanted their boys together. I could have fought back. I could have argued for attending George Washington University. But there was a part of me that liked "easy." There was also a part of me that wanted to make my parents happy. When I was making the decision, I was fine with it. If you questioned me, I would have told you it was my decision and it was a good one. Only through self-introspection can I now admit that I did not realize I was about to start living someone else's dream. I don't blame anyone but myself. It's not like my parents held a gun to my head. Nothing of the sort.

"Easy" can be so enticing. What is (too) easy for you?

Are you a flamethrower or a fire extinguisher?
Flamethrower:
Your children can get As in school and still flunk life.

Fire Extinguisher:
Define your parental job description with care and never waiver from its terms. Through you, they will develop values, social skills and problem solving abilities.

Contemplation Page

How have you helped your children nurture their dreams?

What are the things you believe people are saying about you when you are not in the room? Are you sure?

How have you contributed to making your children unduly dependent upon you? What can you do to give them their independence back?

CHAPTER 9

DEVELOP SHARPER INSIGHTS

Discipline yourself to do the things you need to do when you need to do them, and the day will come when you will be able to do the things you want to do when you want to do them.

ZIG ZIGLAR

At some point in your personal and

professional life, you will be called upon to give an opinion, review a problem, suggest a solution, join in a discussion, clarify your position, debate an issue, support your thinking, comment on a media story, object to an action, present an argument, and or choose a strategy. The circumstances may require a serious, thoughtful and impactful response. Aspects of your career or the continued harmony in a significant business or personal relationship could depend upon responding in an appropriate way, at the right time.

The issues you typically face are rarely about the people in your life. They are about *you*. With this in mind, it is crucial to understand that you may not often see things as they really are. You actually experience events as *you* are. This means that situations are experienced through emotional filters wrapped around belief systems.

You have probably noticed that you perceive circumstances and situations one way if you are happy and content and another way if you are not. Your likes and dislikes have an impact in determining beliefs. Sometimes, a person cannot be dislodged from his or her beliefs. Action will be taken on these beliefs, even though they collide with the truth. What people *believe* to be true is more important than what *is* true.

Ignoring the Decision Process

If you have never adequately considered how to arrive at a sound and reasoned decision, you are not alone. Before delving into the decision making process, it will be instructive to look at objective examples of poor decision making in the business world.

The Quaker company purchased Gatorade in 1983 for $220 million. The Gatorade brand subsequently grew in value to approximately $3 billion. Ten years later, Quaker sought to duplicate that success. The company bought the Snapple brand for $1.8 billion. A mere three years later, Quaker re-sold it for $300 million. This acquisition cost Quaker $1.5 billion.

Its board was relatively silent in its opposition to this sale and did little probing as to the wisdom of such a momentous acquisition.

It is impossible to determine what the board members were really thinking, as the meeting on the Snapple acquisition concluded. However, after the re-sale of Snapple at a staggering loss, it is not too difficult to figure out what individual board members must have been thinking:

"We could have done a lot with $1.8 billion. Other strategic purchases could have been made and plants and equipment could have been upgraded."

"If I had raised an objection, maybe someone else would have joined me to voice a different objection. This would have led to a real discussion, with a different outcome."

"Our expectations were misplaced. We should have delayed the vote when there was no dissenting voice."

"The board's attitude of neutrality was very dangerous. I wasn't sure this was a good move. I should have said something. I should have asked a few questions." Too little, too late.

In another example, Eastman Kodak, with its long and proud history, had several avatars during its existence. A pivotal change occurred when the company invented a roll of film that made it easy for the public to take pictures. For many years, it looked at digital photography but always dismissed it, feeling that the public would never prefer that method over film. Despite opportunities to reverse its decision, Kodak refused to get into digital technology and declared bankruptcy in 2012 after concluding erroneously that the public would never move away from film photography.

If we were to listen to the Kodak board meeting as it weighed in on the superiority of film over digital technology this is what we probably would have heard from its members:

"People love putting film in their cameras."

"Film still provides a better picture than the digital camera."

"Digital photography is a fad. There will always be a huge market for film."

After the bankruptcy filing, the board members were probably thinking differently:

"I should have asked better questions."

"We were so confident that film would always be in demand that we were blind to the obvious and jumped to conclusions."

"I should have challenged these assumptions."

Deeper Thinking

The goal is to always arrive at a reasoned conclusion. This does not guarantee that you will get the result you desire, but it does mean that your decisions will be well thought out *all the time*. Those who are outcome oriented will often be disappointed when that expectation does not materialize. The singular question then becomes, "Did I get what I wanted?" Those with a process in place ask, "Am I making a reasonable and sound decision after considering all the facts and issues?" A person who tries to understand what actually happened is more likely to persevere because he or she will consider where things went wrong and determine whether the issues can be fixed, improved, or tweaked.

Mr. Ziglar would say, "Success is not determined by the hand you were dealt. Rather, success happens when you turn the hand you were dealt into a winning hand. Yearning power is more important than earning power."

In other words, it is far better to be attuned to a world of new possibilities as you work toward the unlimited boundaries of "what could be." Using a consistent process will make that happen. Break things down into small-size components. This makes any task manageable. Outcome-oriented people, always see a mountain, when they could just as easily see a hill. When they are no closer to their goal, they find it impossible to proceed and consequently give up.

When a process is in place, jumping to conclusions will not occur. Every decision will have a failsafe component. Periodically, every decision should be reviewed to determine whether to proceed as planned, or whether modifications need to be considered. Every assumption becomes subject to possible further investigation, as facts and situations change. Whether framing a statement to yourself or to others, you will understand that how you present the same information can elicit different responses. For example, you can say that a surgery has a 85% survival rate or a 15% mortality rate. Each will elicit a different response. The spotlight will also be placed on the idea that some information will always be missing. It's up to you to determine the relevance of the information you would like to have, but may not. You will know the danger of having just one idea on a matter. There is nothing more dangerous than defaulting to that one idea when it's the only one you have.

The Process

The decision-making process that Chip and Dan Heath explain in their book *Decisive* is simple to use and adaptable to any kind of decision you may be called upon to make. Let's examine this four-step process.

    1. It is critical to discover as many options as possible. Typically, as soon as you think you have a viable answer, you stop looking for another possible answer. This is a mistake. You may be missing a better approach to the issue or problem. By initially creating multiple alternatives, finding a better way to proceed won't be overlooked.

    2. You'll then want to decide which option is in fact better. Play *devil's advocate*. Don't make it easy to accept the first idea just because it's *your* first idea. Unearth reasons why additional options may or may not be the better way to go.

    3. In the past, you have probably made decisions you later regretted because raw emotions adversely impacted your decisions. Only upon reflection did you realize a better decision could have been made. When emotions are involved, you need to buy some time. Get a different perspective from those you trust. Another idea is to institute a waiting period that will enable those emotions to dissipate. Most of all, never decide while you are in the grip of strong emotions. Ask yourself: What would (pick a person you admire for sound decision making) do in this situation?

    4. Guarding against overconfidence is key. Think back to some bold predictions that you, (your colleagues, or friends) have made over the years. Upon reflection, you will realize that many of them have been either flat out wrong or could have been improved upon. Consider these common examples: You enter the wrong profession. You want to reverse a tattoo. A "sure thing" business venture fails. You miscalculate how long a home improvement project will take. Now you know that you can protect against poor decision making. Vigilance regarding conclusions and assumptions become

a rather important priority. As you discover new facts and situations, it may be prudent to modify the original thought. Do not close the book on a made decision. Checking on subsequent progress is always a wise thing to do.

Communicating with Ease

Many of these precise decision-making principles also apply to communicating more effectively. Whenever you communicate, you need to question long-held assumptions, develop sound reasons to support your position, evaluate the issue and devise alternative tactics.

Everyone has a belief about something. Turn on any talk show or news program. Watch the guest attempt to support his or her belief. You will discover that many proponents of an issue use unsupportable facts as if they were established truths. However, notice the effectiveness of those who can evaluate supporting reasons, examine different points of view and provide a cogent and logical conclusion. These types of arguments provide "aha" moments.

Providing a logical conclusion takes practice and patience.

For example, look at deeply held beliefs people have on the Second Amendment, abortion rights, or condoms in schools.

Let's address the last one. On this issue, one proponent will forcibly remark that this practice will absolutely reduce teenage pregnancy and the spread of venereal disease. The opposing side will opine that children will abstain from having sex if condoms are not distributed freely. Notice that neither side supported their arguments with facts. Your arguments probably follow a similar pattern.

One reason that this occurs is because many people tend to believe what other people tell them. Everyone develops his or her own team of "authorities," which could be a family member, friend, or colleague. Notice what happens when each side relies on those sources. The argument cannot move forward or conclude. The communication becomes more about whose authorities are better and the real arguments are forgotten.

Circling communication occurs when each side says in effect that "You are entitled to your beliefs and I'm entitled to mine." Notice that there can be no argument or further discussion. Each side merely repeats and reiterates its position. Round and round the non-argument goes. Each side has effectively surrendered its right to articulate and defend a well-thought-out point of view.

Consider your thinking patterns. Thinking precisely is the kind of process that will take you where you want to go. It will get you noticed at work, at school and in the home. Your mind will begin to weigh different points of view. This will require evaluation of the supporting reasons for each point of view. Finally, based upon your examination, it requires a conclusion. However, it is important to note that the conclusion reached today can differ tomorrow because additional facts may appear. When you implement the four-step process, you will see other possibilities you may have ignored. That way, you no longer search for facts just to support your current thinking (confirmatory bias). Your emotions will not unduly influence you; nor will you ignore changing situations. All this can protect you from becoming overconfident in your conclusion.

When you organize your thoughts, you will not depend upon a three-way emotional response: striking out, giving in, or breaking off. You will open a pathway to more options. Things that previously went completely unnoticed will now compete for your attention. You will be transported into a new learning paradigm. Exploration will become a journey of joy.

Make Persuasive Arguments

Perhaps you have heard people say that an argument seems so persuasive. How can you know if it is as persuasive as it sounds? The following suggestions will help:

    1. Be alert for glaring inconsistencies. The more people talk, the greater the chance that their statements contain discrepancies and contradictions. I was at a party recently when someone said, "I always work late into the evening, but last night I left early to see the Knicks play at the Garden." This is an obvious example. Being a good listener is key. Clarity of thought also requires that you dissect the statement for its inherent truth. This exercise is purely logical and you can take the speaker to task. For example, I was recently approached to invest in a real estate deal and was told about all the metrics. It appeared there was a lot of money to be made. I asked one question. "How much are you investing?" and the reply was "My

job is to look for investors. I don't invest in my own projects." This obvious and fundamental contradiction was a red flag. The messenger is hoping you are not listening and will not ask questions.

2. Whenever people are truthful, they are concise and succinct. "If you tell the truth," Mark Twain once said, "you don't have to remember anything." Notice that when people are not telling the truth, their statements are full of useless details. It is almost as if they are trying to convince themselves before doing the same to you.

3. Beware of unsolicited promises. Often the speaker is merely trying to win you over to his or her way of thinking. Whenever the speaker catches a glimmer of doubt in your countenance, the insidious words, "I promise" or "Believe me" are always added.

4. Consider asking additional questions, such as "Does the speaker provide logical evidence that supports his or her assertions?" If the answer is yes, then find out what evidence doesn't support that assertion. How relevant is it? Challenge the assumptions that the speaker makes. When you do, you arm yourself with powerful weapons.

A speaker may employ a few broad tactics to keep an audience off-balance. He or she could resort to name calling for those who oppose his or her viewpoint, use labeling to call out potential foes, criticize differing points of view, or fire back at those who resist the argument with interrogating questions of their own. The purpose of each technique is to make those who are not convinced feel uncomfortable.

Insight Tools to Stay Out of Trouble
Sharp, effective insights reap mighty benefits. You now have the tools to decipher what a speaker is saying and can weigh just how well it is being said. They also provide you with the ability to express your thoughts in a concise and understandable way. As events unfold in your personal and business life, you will be able to determine how to improve the results. Your postmortem tool will allow you to ask the following:

"How did this happen?"
"What can I do now to make this work?"
"How did I contribute to this result?"

You should always ask these three questions. Once you do,

instead of questioning why something didn't work *after* the fact, you are now equipped to ask, "What must be true to make this work *before* its implementation?" This approach applies to projects, friendship and most any relationship.

It is far easier to *stay* out of trouble than to get out of trouble.

MY STORY

I will always remember Mr. Hoffman, who taught history at Roslyn High School. He always tried to get us to understand why and how events unfolded. He felt it was important to understand what our historical subjects were thinking.

He would constantly say, "What people believe to be true is more important than what really is true."

I included these powerful words in Chapter 4 and they are relevant here, too. Years later, after my surgery, I came to realize that he was talking *to* and *about* me. After leaving the hospital, I was having grand mal seizures once a month. The first one occurred in a movie theatre and the second in a restaurant. I came to associate convulsions with public places and refused to go out. The seizures would begin with little notice. One minute everything was fine. Then suddenly an aura enveloped me. It was followed by an intense lightheadedness. This signaled the onset of uncontrollable shaking. My body was not my own. I ceded all control. The electrical switches in my brain went haywire as the neural wiring exploded with excess electrical charges. The shaking and switching lasted for a couple of minutes. I was thoroughly exhausted when the seizure subsided. I felt like I had exercised for hours. On several occasions, vomit would aspirate into my lungs, causing pneumonia. Each time this happened, I wound up in the hospital.

Everyone was quite concerned that I would not leave the house. My dad went into action. Just as he had done research to find an excellent neurosurgeon, he set out on a quest to get his youngest son the psychological help he needed. The power to cure, however, did not reside with the psychiatrist. It was my dad who painted a picture for me that was so real. My recollection does not do justice to the nuance of the story my dad told me, but it is instructive, nonetheless.

Returning from the first and only visit with the psychiatrist, my dad began to tell me the following story as he turned the car onto Exit 39 of the Long Island Expressway:

"There was a young man, about your age, at the golf club, who would go swimming every day. Like you, he also had brain surgery. It was evident that the doctors removed part of his skull. Unlike you, he had a malignant brain tumor. He was dying. He didn't let that stop him from going to the pool. He was determined to enjoy his life for as long as he could. I thought you would want to know how fortunate you really are and that there really is light at the end of the tunnel."

I will remember that story forever because it changed my life. Part of me felt ashamed, while I also felt so fortunate. From that moment on, I was determined to find the strength and fortitude to beat the phobia that had been getting the best of me. The only one stopping me from going out was me. I was afraid if I ventured out I would have a seizure.

What people *believe* to be true is more important than what really *is* true. To test my determination, Shelley and I, along with her parents, went to the movie theatre in Glen Cove. It was a beautiful summer night. To my dismay, the ticket line was wrapped around the block. Sweat began pouring from every pore in my body. Just a week ago, I had refused to leave the house. I was so nervous. Shelley held on to me with a tight, loving grip. She knew I wanted to flee. Her love demanded that I stay. I obeyed. I sat through the entire movie. This, I'm proud to say, was the first of many little successes I would continue to claim. This moment changed what I believed to be true, which is more important than anything else.

I recall the time an organization hired my firm to do all their real estate work. As the work load began, I belatedly discovered that this client really did not match my typical client profile. The prospect of significant legal fees caused me to ignore some disturbing signals. I chose instead, to jump to certain favorable conclusions about the future of this engagement. Sometimes, jumping to the wrong conclusion can be an unpleasant experience. Have you ever jumped to a wrongful conclusion?

Are you a flamethrower or a fire extinguisher?
Flamethrower:
Decisions are made without due consideration for both supporting and opposing points of view.

Fire Extinguisher
A wise and effective decision requires a full and complete analysis of the facts.

Contemplation Page

How many bad decisions would have been avoided if you used a process?

....
....
....
....
....

Why will asking a pre-mortem (before the fact) type question work better than asking a post-mortem (after the fact) type question? How will this benefit you?

....
....
....
....
....

How persuasive are your arguments? What can you do to make them even more persuasive?

....
....
....
....
....

CHAPTER 10
BE IN CHARGE OF YOU

The real opportunity for success lies within the person and not in the job.
ZIG ZIGLAR

Are you drowning in a sea of pain,

disappointment and excuses? Are you giving up because you are uncertain about your next move? At times, you convince yourself that things are getting better—so you talk yourself out of doing something differently. You may think it's best to give things a little more time to develop—and then you wait. Sometimes, the wait can last a lifetime. You wait for a spouse, boss, parent, or government to make the pain go away.

Defining yourself as a victim is the surest way to remain dependent upon others. It is an excuse to do nothing. It is the recipe for refusing to take responsibility for yourself.

"Help me, I can't help myself."
"Help me, I need your attention and love."
"Help me, I am incapable."
"Help me . . . help me . . . help me.
Sound familiar?

Take Control of Your Own Life
Mr. Ziglar often talked about the remarkable tale of the greatest archer of yesteryear, Harold Hill. Despite Hill's remarkable ability, Mr. Ziglar always proclaimed that he could have you hitting the bulls eye more frequently than Harold Hill ever could—that is, providing he blindfolded Hill and spun him around a few times.

Of course you would say something like "How could Harold Hill hit a target he couldn't see?" Here is another question to consider: "How can you hit a target you don't have?" That is the point. You can't take control until you can see your target.

While I am convinced that it is everyone's responsibility to be happy, many have the equation wrong. They either want to be happy all the time or they want others to make them happy all the time.

In Chapter 6, you discovered the significance of action. Since no one is automatically entitled to be happy, it requires that you initiate some form of action so that you can achieve happiness. The journey is the fun, not the destination. Many people get tripped up looking for the outcome instead of the process. If you get a new car, house, job, or raise, you think happiness is guaranteed. Yet, it can be elusive. True and lasting happiness lies within you.

Lead Yourself
From this day forward, dare to dream! You once had dreams and may have simply forgotten them, so why not reclaim them? You can do that by daring to see the vision that you crave for yourself. Become that which you are not, but desperately hope to be.

A Chinese proverb says, "The best time to plant a tree was 20 years ago. The second-best time is today." It is never too late for those seeking their buried treasure.

However, if you find comfort in remaining the victim, you'll also find solace in giving in and giving up. You will never have that *second-best time.*

When your fuel tank of hope is on empty, like a car, you will remain idle. When your fuel tank of hope is full, you can go wherever you desire.

Dr. Seuss said, "You have brains in your head. You have feet in your shoes. You can steer yourself any direction you choose."

Energize your life. Better yet, energize your own life and the lives of those around you. Discover what gives you joy as you embark on the road to becoming who you want to be.

As you attempt to remain in control or take over control, it is important to dispel some of your negative thoughts. Have you ever said any of the following to yourself?

I am not persistent.
I am so afraid of failing.
I am not exciting enough.
I am not strong enough.
I am not smart enough.

On and on it goes. If you have harbored any of these negative thoughts, you're not alone.

Yet, you were born with the ability to persist. Picture yourself when you were an infant. You crawled around on all fours. At some point, you lifted yourself up and fell down. Of course, your next move was to pick yourself up and fall again—and again and again. Each time you tried harder. Once you became good at standing, you were ready to walk. But how could you? After all, you never attempted it before. How could you possibly succeed at something you were attempting to do for the first time? As a young child, you had the gift of persistent-consistency. As a young child, the prospect of *failure* was met with unbridled determination.

Consider a story about Thomas Edison, which has been circulating online for many years and claims to be true. It's not, but nonetheless the mythical version here is still quite instructive.

One day, Edison came home from school with a note from his teacher. His mother opened the note and read it to Thomas. With tears running down her cheeks, she read out loud: "Your son is a genius. This school is too small for him and doesn't have good enough teachers to train him. Please teach him yourself."

And so she did. Luckily, she was trained as a teacher. (This was true.)

Many years later, after his mother passed away and he had already become a great inventor, Thomas came across the original note from his teacher. It said, "Your son is mentally deficient. We cannot let him attend our school anymore. He is expelled."

Edison made the following entry into his diary:

"Thomas A Edison was a mentally deficient child whose mother turned him into the genius of the century." This is where the mythical story ends.

Thomas Edison was later home-schooled by his mother. He was actually labeled addled (confused).

In an interview with *T.P.'s Weekly* in 1907, which is authentic, Edison related what happened that day. He had overheard teachers talking about him and went home crying. His mother took her son back to school and angrily told the teacher he did not know what he was talking about, that Thomas had more brains the he did. Thomas was determined to become worthy of his mother's praise, to show her that her confidence was not misplaced.

Imagine if the online version of the story was true and Mrs. Edison read the note out load, as originally written: "Your son is mentally deficient. We cannot let him attend our school anymore. He is expelled." And likewise imagine, as in the true version of the story, if Mrs. Edison hadn't gone back to the school to challenge the teacher. The effect on young Thomas could have been devastating.

These two versions of the same story, true or otherwise, show the power of words and belief. Nothing has meaning except what *you* give it. What people *believe* to be true is more important than what really *is* true. Even if Thomas was slow and confused in school, he and his mom did not let it define him. His story shows that a positive belief can change anyone's destiny.

When you are not in control of your thoughts, you stop differentiating between failing to do something and calling yourself a failure. When that happens, every failure makes you a failure. When you realize that you *can* control your thoughts, it is important to focus on the choices you have and the consequences that can flow from your decisions.

Control over your life is an awesome task. Possibility thinking creates magic and progress. It helps you realize that every failure does not make *you* a failure. When you stop waiting for things to happen and grant yourself the power to generate action, you will create an escape velocity from any negative thinking that has trapped you.

Being in control is just a choice you make. Start with an easy task. Then build up to accomplishing tougher challenges. Don't be afraid to give yourself a pat on the back along the way. You, and only you, have the power to open the door to opportunity.

It's a choice that *you* make.

MY STORY

As a child, athletics consumed all of my free time. I hated doing anything unless it was related to a sport. I'll never forget one of the biggest epiphanies I ever encountered as a kid. My friend Andy moved from the neighborhood. He was a great guy and an okay athlete. About six months later, Andy's mom dropped him off to visit for the day. A group of us decided to play basketball. Andy was chosen last. Since this was a sport, I didn't have to worry about being chosen last.

The game started. Andy got the ball and hit a jump shot for two points. *Lucky shot,* I thought. Then he took a turnaround jump shot for another two points. Wait, this wasn't the Andy I knew. He dribbled between his legs, took layups with either hand and made us all look like we were playing basketball for the first time. His improvement was miraculous!

Years later, as I became a student of motivation, I always

remembered the show Andy put on that day. It was nothing short of remarkable. Andy had reinvented himself. He had refused to see himself as his friends once saw him—as merely an *okay* basketball player. He became *great*. I learned that if you believe in yourself, you can achieve anything. When you are labeled, you either become the label, or you ignore it. You give in or try harder. Andy taught me that.

After my sophomore year in high school, two sport-related occasions gave me the chance to briefly break the grip of fear. The good thing about fear is that it is not an all-or-nothing proposition. It doesn't have to stop you 100 percent of the time. It is bad enough that it stops you most of the time. When the track coach kept asking me to go out for the team, I finally joined and I also made the varsity football team as a wide receiver. The football coach had encouraged me to try out, even though I was the smallest guy on the team. I didn't last too long. I was injured in the third game and missed the rest of the season.

But I learned something from both of those experiences: Look what happens when you lead and take control. Look what happens when you don't.

I used to care a lot about what others thought and projected my beliefs onto other people. I'm not sure when I gave that up, but now I'm in control.

FEAR: **F**antasies **E**liminate **A**ccurate **R**ealities
False **E**vidence **A**ppearing **R**eal is the commonly accepted version of the classic FEAR acronym. The one I used in its place, more accurately described how I viewed the situation. Accurate realities (objective events & stories) were displaced with misconceptions (perceived stories). I refused to do the following things because I cared too much about what others thought. You see, I usually let my fantasies eliminate accurate realities.

Challenge 1: Play high school baseball.
Fear: Too much competition.
Inner Voice: *If I don't go out for the team, I can't fail.*
Challenge 2: Write for the school newspaper.
Fear: My writing is bad.
Inner Voice: *I don't belong.*

Challenge 3: Run for student office.
Fear: I won't get any votes.
Inner Voice: *Kids will laugh at me.*
Challenge 4: Play a musical instrument
Fear: I'm tone deaf.
Inner Voice: *They think I can't do anything well.*
Challenge 5: Join school clubs
Fear: Nobody wants me as a member.
Inner Voice: *I don't belong anywhere.*
Challenge 6: Audition for school play.
Fear: I won't get cast.
Inner Voice: *I have no talent.*

Taking Control of Your Life Is a Choice

Let's compare this list to accurate realities. There were people hoping I would go out for the baseball team because I could add some talent. My enthusiastic desire to write would have been welcomed. My candidacy for office would have represented a fresh face in the arena of school politics. I have always loved music. Participation in clubs is always welcome. I had a good sense of humor that could have added comedic dimension to the right part in a play.

My detached state of mind throughout high school reflected a safety net of sorts, reflected in that fearful inner voice:

Don't try anything new and you won't get hurt.
Don't attempt a challenge and you can't fail.

What I didn't want to realize then is the other part of the equation:

Don't reach for your possibilities and you will not grow.
Stay away and you will not get smarter and you will not achieve.

Eventually, I learned from Andy's example and from my own trials and tribulations. I came to understand that taking control over my life was a choice I could make.

If you believe, you can achieve.

It took me quite a while to figure out the significance of this idea. How long will it take you?

Are you a flamethrower or a fire extinguisher?
Flamethrower:
Those who are afraid hold themselves back.

Fire Extinguisher:
Only you can overcome *your* fears and lead yourself into your future. Go find it.

Contemplation Page

How do you plan to exert control over your life?

What dreams have you forgotten about? How are you going to transform your hopes into a new reality?

What are you going to do in the next week to demonstrate that **FEAR** can no longer control your thoughts or actions?

CHAPTER 11

UNDERSTAND THE ORIGINS OF FEAR

You are the only one who can use your ability. It is an awesome responsibility.

ZIG ZIGLAR

IF IMPORTANT QUESTIONS AND CONCERNS

about your inner journey remain unexamined, your fears will follow you around like a shadow. At times, your mind will be worrying about what might happen in the future while you waddle in the past, insisting there is little hope. This anxiety-ridden emotional loop will continue unabated if you do not address it.

There are a few things you can do to prevent your fears from gaining the upper hand. It is best to address your fears in two parts— as they pertain to your development and as they pertain to your relationships. With all that you have learned, you can do this now.

I suggest you begin by using failure as motivation and give yourself permission to fail *without* becoming a failure.

"If I'm a somebody when I succeed, then I must be a nobody when I fail."

Sound familiar? You need to guard against thoughts like this. You can't persevere until you see failure as an event. You are not the failure. An allowance must be made for every performance mistake. When you take the time to learn from prior mistakes and improve and do better, you'll start believing that there is always a *next time.*

This is the power of next, which we introduced in Chapter 1. This power allows you to pick yourself up when it's time to perform again. In his book, *Win at Losing*, Sam Weinman suggests that most fears are like a swing and a miss in baseball rather than a commentary on competence. It's what happened in a moment in time. Many people view the swing and a miss as something more negative and sinister. Too many people still believe that they need to get things right the first time. You don't.

Beware of Those Who Wish to Rain On Your Parade

When I was younger, I cared too much about what other people thought and said about me. I was the quintessential example of what Mr. Ziglar called a **SNIOP**—someone who is **S**usceptible to the **N**egative **I**nfluence of **O**ther **P**eople.

According to Mr. Ziglar, a SNIOP is more concerned about pleasing another person than ensuring that he or she is living his or her own life to its fullest potential. As you saw, it took a long time for me to realize that other folks love to pass judgment, make destructive comments and intimidate others.

People love to dump garbage into your mind. They love to rain on your parade because they don't have the possibility of enjoying their own. My own dire negative self-talk only added to the damage.

There are three things you need to correct immediately.

1. Take the power away from those who tear you down.

2. Surround yourself with folks who encourage and support your efforts. Give this power only to people you trust and who genuinely care about you.

3. Talk back to the voice in your head that wants to hold you back. That victory can be achieved because now you know so much more.

Defining Your Integrity

You must be sure about the sustainable values you stand for and live by. In other words, there can be no equivocation. When an important decision has to be made, you and your family can say, "In our home, this is how we do it". You must be committed to this 100 percent of the time. This is *where* and *how integrity* is born. It is about keeping promises and fulfilling expectations. In my professional and family life, my word is my bond. If I say that I will do something, it will be done. I provide sincere praise to others and never criticize them. I criticize the performance, if need be, but not the person. When you are not clear in your behavior, you will become wishy-washy in your thinking and your motives will constantly be questioned.

Should I have done this or that will be your self-talk. When uncertainty creeps in, you will always wonder whether you did the right thing—for yourself and/or others. The aim is to become confidently fearless, not fearful.

Your Mindset: Fixed or Growth?

If you let fear run amuck, every challenge can become a threatening situation. This is especially true if you believe in a fixed mindset. Carol Dweck in her book, *Mindset: The New Psychology of Success*, focuses on the difference between Fixed and Growth mindsets. If you believe that you possess innate intelligence, you are wed to the idea that your intelligence is a static thing you can do little about. This belief reinforces the fragility of your perceived intelligence. If you mess up your ready excuse is that you did not try. Alternatively, you'll blame others or circumstance. This strategy, as far as you are concerned, prevents your intelligence from being called into question.

The brain of someone with a growth mindset works differently. You are always up to the challenge. Your primary goal is to learn. The key difference here is that failure is not the defining moment. It's a problem to learn from. One of the examples Dweck uses is that of Jim Marshall, who played football for the Minnesota Vikings and was involved with one of the most embarrassing plays in the history of the National Football League. He was a defensive player who scooped up a fumble and ran 66 yards - *the wrong way* - scoring for the opposing team.

"It was the most devastating moment of his life," she writes. "The shame was overpowering. But during halftime, he thought, *if you make a mistake, you got to make it right.* 'I realized that I had a choice. I could sit in my misery, or I could do something about it.' Pulling himself together for the second half, he played some of his best football ever and contributed to his team's victory. Nor did he stop there. He spoke to groups. He answered letters that poured in from people who finally had the courage to admit their own shameful experiences. He heightened his concentration during games. Instead of letting the experience define him, he took control of it. He used it to become a better player and a better person."

Determining Your Success

While it is easy to have issues with those you are in close contact with, turning things around is not always difficult. Reframing allows you to turn the nervous energy of fear into usable energy. Fear can be mitigated. Let's consider an example.

Imagine that your job as a salesperson for Company X requires that you call on Mr. Grumpy for an order. Mr. Grumpy is irascible. Because he is so hot-tempered, no other salesperson wants to deal with him. However, you resolve to find a way to interact. On your way over to the company, you decide to act as a resource, to show him how your company can make Company X (Mr. Grumpy's employer) more profitable, productive and competitive. If you can pull this off, Mr. Grumpy will look good to his bosses and you believe, will even treat you differently.

Whenever you refocus your attention on helping an individual perform better, he or she will return the favor tenfold. Being a resource to one in your personal and family life is equally effective. Just substitute profitable, productive, competitive and cost-effective with happy, peaceful, loving and respectful. The key is to look at what others need and help them achieve it.

The War Within
You may point to external events as the culprit for causing your emotional discomfort. You may resent your job, be upset by people in your life, or feel you are being used. However, at the same time, there is also an unnoticed internal war being waged as you confront these external situations. This war is a conflict between your identity (how you see yourself), your relationship with others (how you want it to be) and the desired outcomes you prefer (the resolution of desired issues). External events that you are confronting may leave you dissatisfied because you have not considered the internal conflict being waged within. Determining the answers to the questions below could help resolve inner conflicts as you proceed on your *life's journey*.

1. What keeps you awake at night?
2. If a genie can grant you your deepest wish, what would it be?
3. When folks hear your name, what is the first thing you want them to think of?

The first question focuses upon things that concern you the most. The second question centers on your hopes and dreams and the third may provide solace as you decide just what you want people to say about you when you are gone. Resolving this conflict will provide peace of mind and will dissipate your lingering fear.

Power To Persuade, a book by Jason Frenn, suggests that others can be helped when you are able to understand their internal issues.

MY STORY

My fear became overpowering as I squashed my self-power and authority. I can't count the times I refused to do something because *fear* held me in its treacherous grip. My identity was in serious need of shoring up. In fact, I was stunting my own growth.

The *invisibility shield* required that I remain quiet and innocuous. I never volunteered. When you are young, you learn rather quickly to play the role you are assigned. Speaking of roles, I was chosen to be a rabbit in a school play. I had one line. I didn't want to be a rabbit. But since it was by no means a demanding role, the teacher thought it suited me fine and eventually, so did I.

Until you can look fear in the eye and not blink, you will always be forced back to uncomfortable times. I remember back in 1975 I was regaining my strength after brain surgery and desperately wanted to get out of the house. My dad finally consented to letting me work at his office. The doctors had warned the family how critical it was that I not get upset or become stressed while recovering - that I stay mellow and calm. At the time I started work, my dad was in the process of installing the first computer system in his office. He was anything but calm. The system had its own antiseptic room, with its own air conditioning system. Some mathematical calculations needed to be done, which made me nervous because the surgery had, for the time being, compromised some of my ability to do that quickly. This was my internal battle.

The Manager came into my father's office to meet me. He looked at me and at the huge scar on my head and said, "Can you add numbers?" I was crushed. This 24-year old meekly answered "yes" and stored the anger away. It didn't take much to start doubting myself all over again and revisiting a time I wanted to forget. When I got home that night, I cried like a baby.

The successes I have achieved will never erase the empty feeling of under-achievement I still carry around. Those *what if* thoughts are never too far away from my consciousness. Today, it's not so much about what I've done. It's more about what I could have done. I am now working on that part.

I am no longer controlled by these negative thoughts. Controlled is the operative word. Every now and again, I acknowledge them and move on. It's like saying "Hi" to an old friend as you take a stroll in the neighborhood.

Are you a flamethrower or a fire extinguisher?

Flamethrower:

Worry compounds worry when you fret that your past will repeat itself or that your future will be a repeat of what was.

Fire Extinguisher:

You create raw power over your fear, whenever you commit to take action. When you say, "*Next Time I Will*" fear doesn't have a chance.

Contemplation Page

What keeps you awake at night?

_____
_____
_____
_____
_____

Who make you feel like a SNIOP? List the people you no longer wish to be influenced by.

_____
_____
_____
_____
_____

What three things can you do right now to achieve a growth mindset?

_____
_____
_____
_____
_____

CHAPTER 12
DO LIFE DIFFERENTLY

The basic goal-reaching principle is to understand that you can go as far as you can see, and when you get there you will always be able to see farther.

Zig Ziglar

It is Wednesday, a day like any other,

when the work week is just past the halfway point and you are focusing on the upcoming weekend. For the individual sitting next to you on the train, it is anything but an ordinary day. He's up for a big promotion. It is anything but an ordinary day for the person who was in the elevator with you this afternoon. She is making the sales presentation of her life. It is certainly not an ordinary day for the individual sitting opposite you at lunch. He has decided to tell his adult son that he loves him.

What is the difference among these folks? Why is your Wednesday ordinary, while it holds such promise for these individuals? The answer lies in the difference between penetrating a wall of safety and hiding behind it.

For you, hiding behind the wall has become a daily ritual. You pray for continuity, for sameness, for interchangeable moments that stretch into days, weeks, months and years. Before you know it, decades have passed and you are befuddled that time has flown by.

Again, your focus is wrong. It is not a problem with *time*. It is an insidious problem of opting for *feeling safe*.

Herein lies a great paradox of life. The greatest danger you will ever face is when you inextricably latch on to feeling safe. It is the enemy of the learning paradigm. Your formal education may have ended when you finished school, but learning never does.

Make Magic Happen

When you feel safe you are not learning. You are not growing. Feeling safe is like a never-ending, bright sunny day. The beautiful azure sky beckons all to enjoy. That is the trap. Continuous hot weather will ultimately destroy nature's offerings, if it is not accompanied by precipitation. Likewise, that *safe feeling*, may give you peace of mind at first, but too much of it can be destructive. Living life around the continuous sameness loop of safety sacrifices much. Refusing to take risks may appear to be the prudent choice. Some would argue that ships are safer in the harbor than traveling the seas. And that planes are safer on the ground than flying to a destination.

Mr. Ziglar would counter that this is not the case. Idle ships grow barnacles faster and idle planes quickly begin to rust. Ships were meant to sail and planes were meant to fly and you were meant to achieve your purpose. None of these can happen without a degree of risk.

The good news is, continuous safety loops can be broken at any time. It just requires some words from you:

Today is your day. Break the cycle. Look for the available opportunities others can't see. It's your choice. Are you going to see today as just another typical business-as- usual kind of day, or are you going to think and act differently? Is today the day when you realize exciting possibilities for you and your family?

There may be danger in doing things differently, but there is a lot more danger when you continuously do nothing. Make today the first day of your life. Magic happens when you reach for the stars and develop your talents. Magic happens when you overcome doubts and stretch outside your comfort level. Expanding abilities will attract new opportunities. Success may not happen at that moment. However, if you are persistent, success will eventually be yours.

Beware that success, however you define it, may not happen on your first, second, or third attempt. However, if the passion and desire are there and you choose to learn from each experience, it is just a matter of time until you will snatch that prize of accomplishment in your business, personal and family life. While it's easy to choose to remain in a holding pattern, it is far more difficult (and exciting) to try and reach your potential. Are you ready to blast off?

MY STORY

I look back on my early school years with much regret because aiming low kept me stalled in mediocrity. It caused many possibilities to pass unnoticed and untested. Fear will never get the better of me again. Or, stop me from doing something new. Yes, a poor self-image does take its toll. I once thought that I did not have much of a story. But I do. And so do you.

Eventually, I made magic by just starting! Aiming too low prevents growth. Hitting a low target does not garner any points. Shelley constantly reminded me that it is never too late to achieve and realize one's potential. Detours can make it appear that it is. As long as there is a burning desire, passion and drive to expand one's capabilities, it is never too late. However, a lot of folks just never aim higher. They remain defeated. A *defeated person* is one who has been knocked down and refused to get up. Negativity and self-doubt overpowered the taking of any responsibility for the result. This person will never be aware that another, with the same ugly experience, persevered because of a different belief. Hope is the catalyst that lets you know that "your greatness" could be at the next turn or just over that hill. Winston Churchill said it best. "Never, never, never give up."

Law School sharpened my mind. I could cut any issue and argument to pieces. Brain surgery, paralysis and seizures at age 24 turned my mind into a butter knife. My life was filled with despair, until I stopped holding myself back. I vowed to find my purpose in life. I didn't know that buried treasure could be buried so deep.

Finishing law school, after the surgery, was like going to the gym each day for an exhausting workout. Leaving my father's business to open my law office was the first clue that I could create my reality. I gave my first public presentation on real estate issues. *Doing* can overcome self-doubt. I successfully serviced my first paying client. "I care" is all a client needs to hear.

The American Dream Hour, a weekly radio show with Beverly Bell, my great friend and colleague, was a dream that became reality. I always wanted to have a radio show and I did. I wrote the very first article on reverse mortgages that appeared in the prestigious New York Law Journal. Another thought accompanied by action that was turned into a major achievement.

I entered the mortgage business after closing my law practice. To succeed, you can't be afraid to fail. I authored *Piggy Bank Your Home, Tap into The Power of a Reverse Mortgage.* I kept raising the bar. I authored, with Chase Magnuson, *The Secret Power Behind Real Estate Donations.* Another journey attempted and realized.

It is impossible to have new learning experiences when your life's aim is too low. The key here, I have discovered, is to break free from your zone of comfort. Your greatest days will be in front of you when you can do this. It is a great thing to discover a passion-filled purpose to life. I am doing just that and I do believe I will prevail. I wish the same for you. Are you ready to make the magic happen? Let's do it together.

Are you a flamethrower or a fire extinguisher?
Flamethrower:
The safer you feel, the more endangered you become. You are not growing.

Fire Extinguisher:
When you get that uneasy feeling in the pit of your stomach, it means you are out of your comfort zone. You now have a greater chance of making magic happen in your personal, family and business life.

Contemplation Page

What is the one thing you want to do but can't seem to accomplish?

Do you have a talent you are not developing? What is it? What are you waiting for?

It's "Wednesday." Is it just like any other day? How are you going to make it a special day of achievement?

CHAPTER 13

CLAIM YOUR GREATNESS

*Success is not a destination,
it's a journey.*
Zig Ziglar

THE KEY TO GROWTH AND THE KEY TO WRITING

new chapters about your life are now set before you. You can recapture and/or create your life's story. This book has stripped away some of the mysteries of life and exposed some restraining moorings. You now understand that you have plenary ability to affect your circumstances—for better or for worse. It's a choice that you make.

It's partly a question of how much greatness you are willing to grant yourself. It's also a question of tossing some long-held assumptions into the wind. Both acts take courage. By now, you realize that you cannot change other people. You can only change yourself.

By sharing my story, you have seen a young child grow into a grandfather. While it has taken me many years to overcome my demons, I have won. For the longest time, I didn't know I was possessed with such awesome power. I simply figured things out along the way. I am confident that you can accomplish your task in a fraction of the time and I hope this book helps.

For the most part, we have concentrated on two fundamental areas: Inter-personal and Intra-personal concepts. The former requires an understanding of the needs, concerns and feelings of the other. The latter requires a focus on self-awareness and the responsibilities that it entails. It is critical to possess both abilities.

As I have pointed out, every action is tethered by a thought. The kind of thought you produce will determine how fast and how smooth your ride in the game of life will be. When you come across an obstacle, or bump in the road, you have gathered some ideas that will help you continue on your journey. Many folks get stuck in the quagmire of life and summarily give in and give up when they come up against things they consider inappropriate or unfair. However, you no longer will succumb to the same fate. You can plow through and move forward.

MY STORY

For most of elementary school, I wore the *dunce cap*. It wasn't until fifth grade, when Mrs. Rapp said some kind words to me and the all-too-familiar "I can't" turned into a cautious "I can." I would walk home from school thinking that I couldn't wait for this thing called college, so I could be where no one knew me. Until that time, I felt that I was incapable and unworthy, which made surrendering and crying uncle a painless and quick way to endure the torture I received from my teachers. I seldom raised my hand. In my mind, I made things very simple. God made me an athlete. He didn't make me smart. When it came to playing games outside, I was often chosen first. When it came to playing games inside, like spelling bees, I was often chosen last. In class, I stopped volunteering answers. That way, the class couldn't laugh at me.

When I finally got to Adelphi University, I was determined that things would change. In fact, I vowed that things would be vastly different and better. I learned that I could improve myself by taking concrete actions and making wiser choices. I did not wish to repeat my high school non- involvement stage. The first thing I decided to do was to run for president of my freshman class. I even gave a speech. I was proud of myself. Can you believe the difference a few years make? The election results dictated that there would be a run-off election. Since I received the most votes in the open election, I assumed that I was unbeatable. A funny thing happened when these run-off votes were counted. I lost. Not only did I lose, I received the exact number of votes I received in the open election.

I needed to lose, because my ego, having been held back all those years, was straining to burst loose. There would have been no living with me had I won. Although I didn't know it at the time, losing was good. It made me hungrier. I had a taste of what success felt like. Subsequently, I was elected senator to the Faculty/Student Senate. I was also elected president of my fraternity, Pi Lambda Phi.

Later in life, I knew success required that I always improve my skill level. For example, when I knew I was going to start investing in real estate, I took the Certified Commercial Investment Member (CCIM) coursework to give myself the necessary knowledge. This course is considered by many to be the most comprehensive in the real estate field today.

When I wanted to improve on my sales ability and the ability to skillfully influence others, I enrolled in the Sandler Sales Training course. This helped me a great deal as well.

Taking action is extremely important. Improving my talent not only provided me with knowledge, it also gave me a strategic advantage when analyzing issues. This gave me additional confidence and self-esteem.

A Final Thought

How you respond to your private thoughts makes all the difference in the world. The power of thought can propel you forward, hold you back, or keep you just where you are. The results you achieve depend on whether you are ready to take appropriate action. I like the way Mr. Ziglar illustrates the importance of thoughts by calling them "forerunners of positive action."

That's the key. Anger won't provide additional options. Negative thinking won't solve any problems. When you are down in the dumps, you might say something like, "Look at me, I can't get a break," or "Nobody thinks I can do anything" or I'm not communicating well with the kids."

On and on it may go. While you are busy embracing victimhood, you are not moving forward, that is, unless you choose to take a more positive approach.

Daily Reminders

Before starting your day, here are some simple reminders you should consider each morning. Revisit them each evening as well.
- Always be in *learning mode.*
- Listen carefully. If you do not understand, ask questions.
- Live *your dreams,* not the dreams of others.
- Always test your assumptions.
- Look for meaning in your life. Enjoy the journey.
- Put thoughts into action because thoughts, alone, keep you in neutral.
- Do not doubt that you have Mount Everest-sized talent.
- Your belief system creates or destroys obstacles. It is totally up to you.
- A setback is a setup for a comeback
- It is easier to stay out of trouble than to get out of trouble.

- Overcome your fears. Make mistakes. It could be the best training you'll ever receive.
- Magic happens when you stretch your abilities and step outside your comfort zone.
- Be persistent. You may not succeed the first, second, or third time, but eventually you will.

There you have it. Now go out and harness your power. I can only imagine what you will do if you do *all* you can! You may just claim your greatness and keep it from going up in flames.

Are . . . you . . . ready?

Are you a flamethrower or a fire extinguisher?
Flamethrower:
In spite of all that you have learned, you refuse to apply these fundamental lessons to your life. Remember: Nothing changes if nothing changes.

Fire Extinguisher:
Start with little steps. Internalize the lessons, ideas and concepts in these chapters. And let me be the first to welcome you to the first day of your future.

Contemplation Page

Imagine five years into the future. How will your life change? Provide specific details.

What principle, concept, or idea has impacted you the most?

What questions are you asking yourself that can't be answered in your head? Who can help you with these issues?

My Favorite Zig Ziglar
PRINCIPLES OF LIFE

You are what you are and where you are because of what has gone into your mind. You can change what you are and where you are by changing what goes into your mind.

Man was designed for accomplishment, engineered for success, and endowed with the seeds of greatness.

You were born to win, but to be the winner you were born to be you must plan to win and prepare to win. Then, and only then, can you legitimately expect to win.

With integrity, you have nothing to fear, since you have nothing to hide. With integrity, you will do the right thing, so you will have no guilt. With fear and guilt removed, you are free to be and do your best.

When a company or individual compromises one time, whether it's on price or principle, the next compromise is right around the corner.

Failure is an event, not a person. Yesterday ended last night.

You cannot solve a problem until you acknowledge that you have one and accept responsibility for solving it.

The chief cause for failure and unhappiness is trading what you want most for what you want now.

Be helpful. When you see a person without a smile, give him yours.

You can finish school, and even make it easy—but you never finish your education, and it is seldom easy.

Many marriages would be better if the husband and wife clearly understood that they are on the same side.

Other people and things can stop you temporarily. You are the only one who can do it permanently.

Positive thinking won't let you do anything, but it will let you do everything better than negative thinking ever will.

Acknowledgments

Only with the help of other special folks has *Don't Play with Fire* seen the light of day.

Jerry Allocca, an incredible teacher, whose course I took at Hofstra University, provided pearls of wisdom, laser-like recommendations and insightful guidance. I especially appreciated his faith and confidence that this book could be something special.

Jennifer Truitt, Executive Director of Ziglar Family is also a Ziglar Legacy Certified Trainer and Coach. She is a woman of unbounded intelligence, warmth and energy. She offered many insightful suggestions and was totally unafraid to tell me that certain content was not as clear or as powerful as I initially believed them to be.

David Tabatsky, a word meister, can give deeper meaning to any thought or idea and presents them in a more compelling way. He made sure that the text and my message was clear and concise.

Jan Guarino is a graphic designer extraordinaire. She can take a concept, make it better and put it into a magnificent design. The idiom, a picture is worth a thousand words aptly describes the depth of her ideas and designs.

And then there is my extended Ziglar family in Dallas, Texas. You stir my heart with your respect, kindness and caring. You elevate all who walk through your doors.

And to all those incredible folks who I was so fortunate to meet at the Ziglar programs, I thank you for your inspiration.

Speaking of inspiration, I must share a few words about my family.

I thank Shelley for her invaluable suggestions, her insights and patience during the initial writing and re-writing stages. She was happier than I, when the book was finally completed. She gave me the strength to weave my story into a compelling narrative. Without this woman by my side, I would not know how to love nor how to believe in myself.

As I put pen to paper, I often thought about the kind-hearted principles Jason and Cory embody. They also evince a rock-solid belief that nothing comes before family. Each has found their way.

It's not what they do, it's how and why they do things that makes me so proud.

Of course, a bunch of the credit goes to Cory and Blair, our daughters-in-law. They have made our boys the happiest men on the face of the earth in a home-filled with love, caring and respect. All great things start in the home.

My thoughts often drifted to the grandchildren-Makayla, Lexie and Mason. I picture lives filled with hope and incalculable promise. I can only imagine what they would do if they did all that they can.

I love you all.

About the Author

Dennis is among the relatively few Ziglar Legacy Certified Trainers who is a Ziglar Legacy Certified Coach. He is also A DISC Certified Human Behavior Consultant. Having survived serious illnesses and challenging life issues, Dennis is keeping his vow to do something special with his life. His journey of self-discovery and his original search for that purposeful and meaningful life were met with intractable restraining forces, which took years to overpower. Along the way, he learned mighty lessons that have transformed his personal, business and family experiences. He is living now as if he is living life for a second time. This time, however, he is wiser and smarter and wishes to help you achieve the same success.

Dennis has provided a spark that has helped his peers with sound business and personal advice. Today, he has refined his methods and is helping others find meaning, direction, accomplishment and success in all areas of their lives.

He follows the teachings of the iconic Zig Ziglar, who helped over 250 million people get everything they wanted out of life. Mr. Ziglar is considered one of the greatest motivators, teachers and success mentors of all time and has published 32 books.

Dennis is a prolific writer. He has authored two other business/legal books, *(Piggy Bank Your Home: Tap into the Power of Reverse Mortgages* and he co-authored *The Secret Power Behind Real Estate Donations* and has been a contributing author to the *CPA's Guide to Long Term Care Planning* and *Happily Ever After.... Expert Advice for Achieving the Retirement of Your Dreams.* Additional motivational and self-improvement thoughts appear at www.dennishaber.com. along with the *Don't Play With Fire E- Workbook.*

WAYS TO BRING DENNIS' WISDOM TO YOU

Dennis has created multiple platforms for further exploration of the Ziglar principles found in this book. They include the following:

E-Workbook:
Continue on your journey towards greatness with these supplemental materials.

Webinar:
Dennis presents material from the book in an online "classroom" setting.

Keynote Speaking:
Don't Play With Fire comes to life when Dennis delivers one of his inspirational presentations. His speeches are designed to engage and empower audiences to turn high volume negative thoughts into unstoppable and repeatable successes.

Individual Coaching:
Your journey begins with a customizable 12- or 24- session package. We help you get where you want to go. This co-creative, proven process will identify your skills, capabilities and the untapped potential that resides within you. We offer support and accountability, as we coach you through the resolution of existing issues.

Workshop:
For those who prefer a group setting, a live workshop provides a great interactive experience. It allows for additional feedback as you proceed on your journey to increase productivity, harness potential and improve important relationships. These programs can be hosted at corporate headquarters, community centers or at other convenient venues.

For more information, please visit:
www.Dennishaber.com
and you can contact Dennis Haber at:
Dennis@Dennishaber.com
516-822-1020

LIFE IS A TEAM SPORT

The game of life is a team sport. As with any team sport, it takes an organization, working in solidarity with its members, to achieve over the top success. The members of a team always include the same grouping of supporting individuals: Teammates, coaches and cheerleaders.

Imagine how quickly the desired results can be reached when your teammate, coach and cheerleader are the same person. Dennis Haber, as your teammate, coach and cheerleader will provide never ending enthusiastic encouragement; will share your commitment to succeed; will motivate you to exceed your expectations; and he will keep your spirits raised as you knock down and eventually knockout your unyielding opponents of life: Fear, adversity and self-doubt.

Dennis learned how to overcome and battle through life's obstacles by trial and error. It has taken him years to triumph over his personal challenges. He offers you a much faster path to achieve the life of your dreams.

His speeches will propel you into the future so you can look back and catch a glimpse of how great life can be. He will have you clamoring for more as he shows you how to activate the **TRIPLE A PIVOTAL SECRETS FOR SUCCESS**. His business and personal workshops provide profit driven methods for improving the bottom line in the workplace and contain mountain sized principles for improving life at home. His private coaching strategy sessions offer confidential feedback with action plans for sustained results.

Victimhood will become a thing of the past. Staying in a rut will become a thing of the past. That feeling of hopelessness will become a thing of the past. You will finally be able to take control over your greatest asset, your life.

Succeed today. Win tomorrow. Prosper forever.

Imagine finally having:
    Peace of Mind
    Financial Security
    Abundant Success
    Bountiful Health
    Abiding Respect
    A Life Filled with Hope

Imagine holding on to that cherished job
Imagine improving your marriage
Imagine improving your relationships with your kids
Imagine getting that promotion
Imagine acing that speech and presentation and
Imagine dealing successfully with life's many unannounced surprises.

Don't you owe it to your family and to yourself to become the person you were meant to be; to do all the things in life you have dreamed about; and to have everything life should offer? Well you can if you are willing to do some work. Make that call or email Dennis Haber today.

OUR BETTER THAN RISK FREE GUARANTEE
For any workshop or coaching engagement, no fee is due until after the first session of the workshop or coaching session has occurred. If you are not satisfied, no payment is due and the engagement shall be cancelled without further liability.

www.ingramcontent.com/pod-product-compliance
Lightning Source LLC
Chambersburg PA
CBHW070607010526
44118CB00012B/1464